CASE STUDIES IN
CULTURAL ANTHROPOLOGY

GENERAL EDITORS
George and Louise Spindler
STANFORD UNIVERSITY

BUNYORO
An African Kingdom

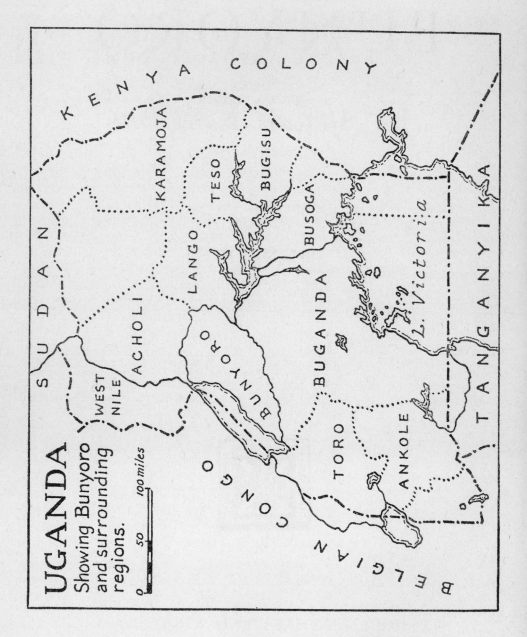

UGANDA
Showing Bunyoro and surrounding regions.

0   50   100 miles

KENYA COLONY

SUDAN

KARAMOJA

TESO

BUGISU

LANGO

BUSOGA

ACHOLI

WEST NILE

BUNYORO

BUGANDA

L. Victoria

TORO

ANKOLE

TANGANYIKA

BELGIAN CONGO

BUNYORO

An African Kingdom

BY

JOHN BEATTIE

Oxford University

HOLT, RINEHART AND WINSTON

NEW YORK   CHICAGO   SAN FRANCISCO   TORONTO   LONDON

About the Author

JOHN BEATTIE received his D.Phil. in social anthropology from Oxford University, where he has taught since 1953. Previous to that he had taught philosophy at Trinity College, Dublin, for two years and then served as a district officer in Tanganyika for eight years before deciding to become a professional anthropologist. He is interested in philosophy, the methodology of the social sciences, and the ethnography of East Africa. He has published a number of theoretical papers as well as articles on aspects of Nyoro social life.

About the Book

This book is many things. It is a study of a feudal East African kingdom, with parallels to the England of William the Conqueror. It tells us of the conflict between feudal and bureaucratic administration and of that between European and traditional Nyoro standards of behavior. History can be important not only for the great civilizations, but also for the simpler, smaller-scale societies; this book amply demonstrates that this is true of the Nyoro. In their history, myth is transitional to fact, starting eighteen royal generations ago and continuing through 1862, when the grandfather of the present king was on the throne and the explorers Speke and Grant arrived on the scene, to the present, where the consequences of this history are seen in the present circumstances of the Nyoro people. But most importantly, this book is a case study of contemporary social relations within a complex and changing East African society. The social behavior of the Nyoro is analyzed in various significant dimensions—at the level of political action and legal control, in relationships between neighbors and between man and the supernatural, and within the system of reciprocal kinship obligations. Dr. Beattie has provided us with an unusual combination of historical perspective and functional analysis of a social system.

GEORGE AND LOUISE SPINDLER
General Editors

Stanford, California
December 1959

Foreword

THE FIELDWORK on which this book is based was carried out under the auspices of the Treasury Committee for Studentships in Foreign Languages and Cultures, London, and I owe much to their generosity and to the freedom they allowed me in planning my research. I spent altogether about twenty-two months in Bunyoro, spread over the years 1951 to 1955, living with the people and, after the first six months or so, working through the Nyoro language. For most of the time I employed one or two Nyoro research assistants, who were particularly helpful in assisting me to carry out detailed household and genealogical surveys in the four villages which I studied intensively. In obtaining information about the career histories of chiefs and about types of land holding I made use of a stenciled questionnaire form, and I had household survey forms printed, for use as a comprehensive *aide-mémoire* rather than as a formal instrument of research. I also invited literate Nyoro to write essays on topics selected by me, and awarded cash prizes for the best. I am greatly indebted to the many people who submitted long and interesting essays, and also to the eminent Nyoro who helped me to judge them.

In carrying out fieldwork one incurs obligations to a great many people. I cannot acknowledge more than a few of these here, but I must record the willing help of the Mukama of Bunyoro, Sir Tito Winyi Gafabusa IV, C.B.E., and of many members, past and present, of his Native Government. I and my family also received much assistance and kindness from officers of the Protectorate Administration and their wives, also (and especially) from the representatives of the Church Missionary Society at Hoima. From the Director and members of the East African Institute of Social Research at Makerere College, Kampala, I received both hospitality and intellectual stimulus in generous measure. But my greatest field obligation is to my Nyoro assistants, and above all to the very many individual Nyoro of all classes who were my friends, companions, and teachers. If any of them should read this book, I should like them to know that I am well aware that no foreigner can hope in the brief period of something less than two years to acquire a full under-standing of the whole culture of another people, especially one as rich and complex as that of Bunyoro. I am not so arrogant as to claim to have done so. If I have learned something of a few of Bunyoro's most important social in-stitutions and values, and if in the following pages I have succeeded in com-municating some of this limited understanding to others, I have done all that I could have hoped to do.

Dr. John Peristiany, Professor I. Schapera, Dr. H. Meinhard, and Dr. Audrey Richards have commented helpfully on earlier drafts of various parts of this book. For valuable criticism of the present draft I am particularly indebted to my teacher, Professor Evans-Pritchard, and to Dr. R. G. Lienhardt and Dr. Rodney Needham.

J. B.

Oxford, England
December 1959

Contents

King (Mukama) of Bunyoro in front of one of his "palace" buildings.
(Photo: Department of Information, Uganda Protectorate.)

Family with traditional beehive-shaped house.

Banana beer being trodden out in banana grove.

Family with modern mud-plastered and iron-roofed house.

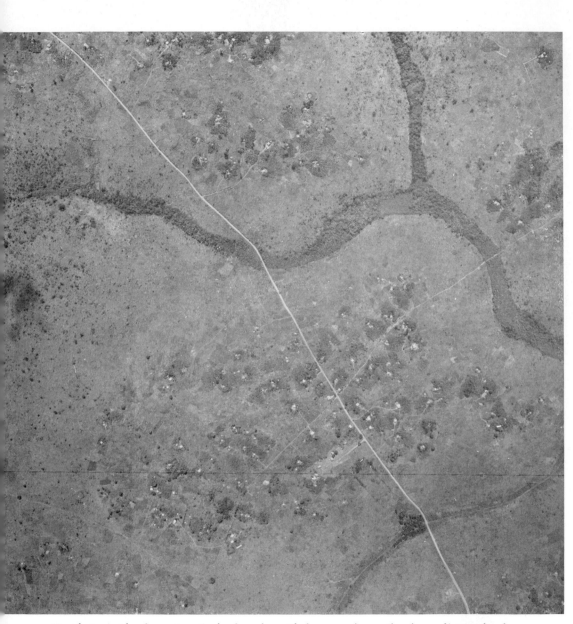

Air photograph of comparatively densely settled area a few miles from district head-quarters, intersected by motor road. Note especially disposition of homesteads and gardens on raised areas separated by swampy streams. Scale approximately 3½ inches to one mile. (Photo: Hunting Aerosurveys Ltd.)

Introductory

THIS BOOK is intended to provide a brief general introduction to the social life of the Nyoro, a Bantu-speaking people who live in a fertile country of small hills and swampy valleys in the uplands of western Uganda, in east central Africa.[1] They number about 110,000, and occupy a region of about 4,700 square miles, so their country is not densely populated, less so in fact than the neighboring kingdoms of Buganda, Toro, and Ankole. But Nyoro are not evenly distributed over their territory; most of them live in fairly closely settled areas, separated by wide stretches of uninhabited bush. Though they do not live in compact villages, as some African peoples do, their homesteads, which typically consist of one or two mud-and-wattle houses around a central courtyard, surrounded by banana groves and food gardens, are rarely more than shouting distance from at least one neighbor. Every Nyoro belongs to one of a number of exogamous, totemic clans, membership of which is acquired in the paternal line.[2] But as these do not form distinct local groups, a man's neighbors generally include unrelated persons, as well as kinsmen and relatives-in-law.

Long ago Nyoro had great herds of cattle. But these have been practically wiped out by war and disease, and there are now only a few thousand

---

[1] Nyoro speak of themselves as *Banyoro* (singular Munyoro), their language as *Lunyoro,* and their country as *Bunyoro.* I omit the prefix, except in the last case, in the interest of simplicity.

[2] *Exogamous* (substantive *exogamy*) means "marrying outside," and implies that marriage is forbidden within a specified group, usually though not necessarily a *clan.* *Totemism* (adjective *totemic*) usually refers to a ritual association between specific social groups in a society (usually *clans*) and specific animate or inanimate objects, which are called *totems.* Where (as in Bunyoro and elsewhere in Africa) members of totemic groups are required to respect and to avoid injuring the totemic species, we may speak of *totemic avoidances.* A *clan* is usually a named group of people who believe themselves to be descended in one line (that is, either through males only or females only) from a common ancestor in the remote past. Members of the same clan usually have special obligations toward one another.

head, mostly in a favored corner of the country which is free from tsetse fly, carrier of the fatal cattle disease trypanosomiasis. At the present time the typical Nyoro is a small farmer, who cultivates from four to eight acres of land, and owns some goats and chickens and perhaps a few sheep. For food he grows millet (the traditional staple), sweet potatoes, cassava, and different kinds of peas and beans. Bananas he uses mainly for beer making. He grows cotton and tobacco as cash crops, and in a good year these may bring him two hundred shillings or more.[3] Some Nyoro are itinerant traders and shopkeepers, but most trade is still in the hands of the immigrant Indian community, as in other parts of East Africa.

Though Nyoro are not wealthy, they are not badly off by East African standards: most people have some good clothes, many have bicycles, and some own cars and lorries. In 1953 Nyoro men paid annual local and government taxes amounting to about 26 shillings. There are good main-road communications in the kingdom, and innumerable cycle paths and tracks. The main towns of Hoima (the capital) and Masindi have hospitals, and there are dispensaries at various points in the district. Education is almost wholly in the hands of the two main Christian missions, the Native Anglican Church (associated with the Church Missionary Society) and the Roman Catholic White Fathers. Literacy in Bunyoro is estimated as between 30 and 40 percent over the age of ten, but as yet only a minority of school children read beyond primary level.

Bunyoro is almost wholly "African." There are about 800 Indians, mostly engaged in retail trade. Only a few square miles are alienated to nonnatives, mostly Indians. The hundred and forty or so Europeans are mostly employees of the Railways and Harbors administration, which handles the considerable traffic which passes between Uganda and the Sudan, via Lake Albert and the Nile. The British government, which administers the whole of the Uganda Protectorate, is represented in Bunyoro by a district commissioner stationed at Hoima, and two or three assistants. There are also a few departmental officers, responsible for agriculture, veterinary matters, police work, fisheries, and so on. But the indigenous Nyoro people form the mass of the population.

The Bunyoro native government operates under the general supervision and control of the British administration. At its head is the hereditary ruler of Bunyoro, the king or Mukama. Nowadays he is advised by a central secretariat, consisting of a prime minister, a chief justice, and a treasurer. He is the head of a graded hierarchy of territorial chiefs, of whom the most important are the four county chiefs, each responsible for one of the four districts into which the country is divided. Beneath them are the subcounty chiefs, and below them again are the "parish" chiefs and the village headmen. So Bunyoro is, as it is said always to have been, a centralized, hierarchically organized state, with the Mukama at the apex of the pyramid of traditional authority, and the hundred and fifty or so village headmen at its base. In pre-European

---

[3] The shilling, made up of a hundred cents, is the standard coin in East Africa. Twenty of them make a pound. Approximately seven shillings equal one American dollar.

times the Mukama was thought of as the ultimate source of all political authority; nowadays everybody knows that he is subject to the superior authority of the European administration. This of course has important effects on traditional attitudes toward the Mukama and his chiefs.

Not much can be said of Nyoro origins. The orthodox view is that the original inhabitants of the country were negroid agriculturalists, and it is supposed that the impact on these of successive waves of immigrants, some at least of whom were pastoral, has resulted both in the wide range of physical type and in the strongly marked distinction between rulers and ruled which are now characteristic of the peoples of this part of Africa. Throughout this region the pastoral Hima invaders (called Huma in Bunyoro) assumed the role of overlords, dominating the indigenous Iru, or peasant peoples, who form the governed majority. But for Bunyoro this is an oversimplification. Although the cattle-herding Huma have always regarded themselves as superior to Iru, in Bunyoro the matter was complicated many generations ago by the arrival from the north of the Nile of a third element, the Bito, whose affinities are with the non-Bantu Acholi and Alur of present-day Uganda. These darker-skinned Nilotic invaders took over the Nyoro kingship from an earlier dynasty, and the present Mukama claims to be the twenty-sixth Bito king. Much of the prestige and authority associated in the more southerly kingdoms of the region (which the Bito did not reach) with the Hima attaches in Bunyoro to the Bito, especially to members of its royal lineage.[4] But although status distinctions are strongly marked in Bunyoro, we do not find there the rigid, castelike discrimination described for some neighboring peoples such as the Ankole, and it has always been at least theoretically possible for able Nyoro commoners to rise to positions of high authority in the state.

Nyoro believe that their kingdom was once much greater than it is now, and that their Mukama is the direct descendant in the male line of the ancient rulers of an empire which extended over most of present-day Uganda and perhaps beyond it. We cannot now say much about this ancient state, or even be quite sure that it ever existed, but we may be certain that if it did it was not a compact political unit, but rather a loose association of semi-independent states connected with the central kingdom through the sporadic payment of tribute. It is certain, however, that in historical times Nyoro territory has been much reduced both by the British and by the neighboring Ganda. Nyoro are very conscious of their former greatness, and we shall find that present-day Bunyoro cannot be understood unless we know something about its traditional political system and about the historical events that have befallen it. For the past determines the present, and attitudes and values which were appropriate to the traditional system still survive in the radically altered social and political scene of today.

---

[4] A *lineage* consists of all the descendants in one line (that is, either through males only or through females only) of a particular person through a specified number of generations. It differs from a *clan* in that while usually all the members of a lineage know exactly how they are related to all the other members of it, and together they often form a corporate group, clan members may not be able to trace genealogical links with other clan members, and often clansfolk are widely dispersed.

These are some of the elementary and essential facts concerning the people whom this book is about; it may still be asked "What are Nyoro really like?" We shall be better able to answer this question, if it is the kind of question that can be answered at all, at the end of our study of their social institutions. But a good many Europeans, from the time of the first contacts just a century ago until the present, have passed judgment on Nyoro character, and it is a fact of considerable anthropological interest that almost all of these judgments have been unfavorable. Thus a nineteenth-century writer described the Nyoro (whom he had never seen) as "mean, grasping and selfish"; a lady missionary reported that work was repugnant to them and that nothing attracted them irresistibly save indolence and ease; and officials and missionaries have referred from time to time to their "apathy," "decadence," "habits of intemperance," and "evident sense of inferiority." Usually assertions like these tell one more about the persons who make them than about the people they are made about. In any case it is the existence and origin of such opinions, rather than their truth or falsehood, that interest anthropologists. I must say here, however, that I found Nyoro to be very courteous, hospitable, and generous people. Most of them are quick witted, thoughtful, and humorous, and many have in recent years achieved high distinction by European standards.

But there is still in Bunyoro a widespread underlying fear and distrust of Europeans. This is rarely explicit, and certainly there is no overt hostility: relations between individual Europeans and Nyoro are usually good and often excellent. But it is widely believed among the less educated majority that Europeans dislike Nyoro and are hostile to their interests, and this is bound to lead to some mutual distrust and suspicion. Some of the grounds for this belief are considered in Chapter 2. Though I lived in close social contact with Nyoro, and have many Nyoro friends, very few trusted me completely (why should they?), and those who did were mostly younger men. Right up to the end of my stay in the country many of my best friends continued to deny firmly that such things as sorcery and divination could possibly occur nowadays, despite ample and continuous evidence to the contrary. They knew, of course, that I knew about these things, but it was better not to talk about them. We shall see why when we come to Chapter 7.

There are many good reasons why the kingdom of Bunyoro is worth studying, but four of them are especially relevant here. The first applies to all studies of peoples remote from ourselves. It is that we have here a community of real people, who have, so far as we can tell, pretty much the same innate constitution and capacities as any other people, and yet who have developed their own distinctive social system and way of life. As members of the same human family, we are bound to be interested in the very different ways of life which other peoples have worked out for themselves. And in the case of preliterate or only recently literate societies, our interest must be an urgent one, for rapid industrial and technological advance are quickly destroying or altering many of them, so that soon perhaps there will be none of them left to study.

Turning from general considerations to more particular ones, a second reason why Bunyoro is worth studying is just because it is the kind of kingdom it is. Although it is changing rapidly, it still preserves many of the characters of a centralized, "feudal" state, oddly reminiscent in many ways of the feudal kingdoms which existed centuries ago in Europe and elsewhere. I use the word "feudal" here in its simplest sense, to refer to the kind of political system which is based on the relation between a superior and his inferior or vassal, where the latter holds lands, and authority over the people living on these lands, "in feud" from the former. This means that the vassal must render homage and services of various kinds (the onus of which will chiefly fall on his peasant dependants) to the superior lord from whom he holds his lands and authority. Traditional Bunyoro has many features in common with such a system, and we shall find that many attitudes and values appropriate to it still survive in present-day Bunyoro, though not always very harmoniously. Thus a second reason for studying Bunyoro is that it has, or had until quite recently, a type of social structure having many points of resemblance with kinds of societies known to us in history. Perhaps we may acquire a clearer understanding of certain features of our own historical past by studying such present-day "feudal" states as Bunyoro.

But Bunyoro, like other recently preliterate societies, is undergoing radical change as a result of contact with a powerful and complex Western culture, and this is a third reason why it should be studied. A living culture is always something more than "a thing of shreds and patches"; in at least some respects it is a systematic whole, as we indicate by giving it a name. This does not mean that its parts all fit neatly together like the pieces of a jigsaw puzzle, as certain "functionalist" anthropologists seem sometimes to have supposed. In times of change it often happens that incompatible beliefs and institutions come to coexist, and when this happens various kinds of conflicts may arise. This has occurred in Bunyoro as it has in other societies; perhaps more acutely than in most. So here we can write an actual case history of social change; we can record what happens when a coherent social system is subjected to the often disruptive impact of European civilization.

The fourth important reason for studying Bunyoro is its ethnographic representativeness. Almost the whole of the vast region between the great lakes of Victoria, Albert, and Tanganyika is occupied by centralized native states; these vary greatly in size but have very similar constitutions. They are all hereditary monarchies; they all have strongly marked, sometimes extreme, distinctions of class and status; and they are all hierarchically organized. All these peoples speak related Bantu languages, and it has become usual in ethnographic literature to refer to them collectively (and also to a few other peoples in the area who traditionally lack centralized government) as the interlacustrine Bantu. Although Bunyoro differs from some of these states in important respects, it resembles them in many more, and may even be said to be typical. So in studying Bunyoro we are not simply studying a unique culture, though one with historical analogues: in analyzing it we are informing ourselves of many of the essential characters of the type of native states which have for centuries occupied this vast and populous region of Africa.

These are some reasons why it is worthwhile to learn about Bunyoro; it remains to make clear what kind of study is proposed for this book. Since anthropology means different things to different people, it is important that the author make clear what he is attempting. The first thing that must be said is that since this book is written by a social anthropologist, it will be mostly about social relations; that is, about the ways in which Nyoro generally behave towards and think about one another. The word "generally" is important: the social anthropologist is not interested in every social relationship that he can discover, only in those which are "institutionalized," standardized, and hence characteristic of the people being studied. In Bunyoro, as in every other society, there are special patterns of behavior and special attitudes and ways of thinking which are held to be appropriate in dealings between people who belong to certain categories (such as chiefs, diviners, clansmen, strangers, fathers, sons, neighbors, and so on). If this were not the case, ordered social life would be impossible, for people's behavior would be unpredictable. We may say that in our study we are primarily concerned with the statuses and roles which are characteristic of Bunyoro. We are interested in the kinds of people there are and the kinds of things they are expected to do, rather than in the particular individuals who happen to occupy particular statuses at a particular time. Of course we are interested in real people (these are the raw material of our study), but our concern is with what these real people share with other real people—that is, with their common culture, rather than with what is unique and peculiar to them as individuals. And this common culture includes their shared framework of social relations, and their beliefs and values. It is because this book is centered on social relations that its four central chapters are concerned respectively with the king, the chiefs, relatives, and neighbors. For relationships centering on some or all of these four categories of persons comprise for most Nyoro practically the whole ambit of their social life.

A concern with social relations does not, however, imply neglect of "culture." No adequate description of a social relationship can omit reference to the ideas and beliefs which the parties to it have about themselves and about one another; this kind of mental content is a large part of what culture means. The main focus of our interest will be in social relationships, but we shall be concerned with other aspects of Nyoro culture insofar as they help us to understand these relationships. Thus Chapter 2 deals with the past and with Nyoro ideas about it, rather than with contemporary social relationships, for we cannot fully understand the latter unless we know something about Nyoro history and their ideas about it. In the same way, Nyoro beliefs about the supernatural, discussed in Chapter 7, are cultural data, but we shall see that many of them play a very important part in interpersonal relations. Though a good deal has been said and written about the difference between culture and society, it is really very much a question of relevance; to give a coherent account of anything it is necessary to deal with it from one point of view at a time, and in this book we study the kingdom of Bunyoro primarily in its aspect as a working system of interpersonal relations.

I have said that our study is of present-day Bunyoro; strictly speaking it is of Bunyoro as it was during the years from 1952 to 1955, when I was there. This book does not attempt to reconstruct a traditional past which no longer exists. But we can understand the present situation better if we know something of how it came to be as it is. This is one reason why social anthropologists should not, and usually do not, neglect history. They are not historians; they do not seek to understand the past for its own sake. They are concerned with it only when it can be shown to be directly relevant to the understanding of the present. In some simpler preliterate societies there *is* no history to be studied prior to the very recent impact of Western civilization; there are no written records, and the past is seen as differing from the present only in respect of the individuals who occupy the different roles in the society, which themselves continue unchanged. And where there is no history, of course it cannot be studied. But Bunyoro has a history of contact with Western culture now almost a hundred years old, as well as its own traditional dynastic history which stretches back through the centuries. We cannot afford to neglect it.

But there is another sense in which history may be important, and this is in its aspect not as a record of past events leading up to the present, but rather as a body of contemporary ideas about these past events. This is what the English philosopher Collingwood aptly called "incapsulated history," because these ideas are contained in and so form a part of contemporary social attitudes and relationships. We shall find that Nyoro ideas about the history of their relations with Europeans differ in some important respects from European ideas about the same history. It might even be said that there are two histories of these events, and if we are to understand how present-day Nyoro think about themselves and about Europeans we shall have to know something about them both.

Two more introductory themes must be considered briefly before we go on to the detailed story. The first of these relates to the problem, which faces every modern anthropologist, of translating the essentials of one culture into terms of another culture, his own. The earlier anthropologists (with some notable exceptions) were hardly aware of this problem; they were mostly content to record their findings in their own cultural terms, for their knowledge of the people they wrote about was rarely deep enough for them to see that often this approach involved gross misrepresentation. Nowadays the position is very different. Advances in field techniques, and in the depth and extent of the knowledge so gained of hitherto little-known peoples, have highlighted this communication problem. It has become increasingly plain that although there is a great deal that is common to all cultures everywhere (if this were not so, no understanding would ever be possible at all), there are also very many significant and subtle differences in the ways in which different peoples "factor out" their universe. This means, of course, that in every culture there are concepts which do not have any exact equivalent in another culture, so that any translation is bound to be to some extent a mistranslation. We shall see in Chapter 5, for example, that since many of the categories of Nyoro kinship terminology have no exact equivalents in English, to translate them by familiar English kinship terms may lead to serious misunderstanding. There is no easy solution to this problem; I have to write my book in English and not in Nyoro. But it is important to be alert to the possibility of misunderstanding arising from this fact. I shall try to avoid misrepresentation as much as I can by presenting Nyoro categories of thought and behavior as far as possible as they conceive them, even if this sometimes involves circumlocution. Only thus may we hope to gain some idea of what their own social and cultural system means to Nyoro.

This leads to my last introductory point, which is an attempt to answer the question: What are the basic values of Nyoro society, in terms of which their social and cultural life makes sense? It might be thought that this question rightly belongs at the end of our inquiry, not at the beginning. But the wholeness of Nyoro social life will emerge more clearly if we know from the beginning what its most striking features are. We must remember that a book is not itself a social study; it is only a report on one. For me the salient features of Nyoro culture emerged only after many months of fieldwork, but the reader is not required to retrace with me this long and sometimes tedious process; my responsibility to him is to present my findings as clearly and accurately as possible. There are two associated concepts which I believe to afford the key to Nyoro culture, and in presenting my material in the following pages I shall be particularly concerned with them. The first of these is the distinction between the superimposed, centralized, pyramidal state on the one hand and the relatively homogeneous, closely knit community on the other; the second is the pervasive concept of superordination and subordination— the notion that some people are always above others, and some people always below.

The first of these notions, the distinction between state and community, has long been familiar to sociologists. It is a distinction which Nyoro themselves often make quite explicitly. For them, social relationships fall broadly into two categories. First there is the system of political relations (concerned with territorially based power and authority) which centers on the kingship and the hierarchical system of chiefs. This is the realm of the state, which sociologists regard as a particular kind of association, concerned with the maintenance of public order through an organized system of authority. It is not at all the same kind of thing as a community, which comprises a great number of different kinds of associations, directed toward different ends. The state is a political entity, and it is defined in terms both of the end to which its activities are directed (the maintenance of order in a certain region) and of the means which it uses for this purpose (which usually include the use or threat of force by an accepted authority, such as a king or chief). Nyoro often speak about the state, in contradistinction to the local community of neighbors and kinsmen, and when they do so they are referring to their relations with the chiefs, of whatever ranks, or with the Mukama himself. The words they use for this political or "statal" dimension of their social life are *bukama* and *bulemi,* which we may translate respectively as "kingship" and "govern-ment." But at once we are faced with the difficulty of translation which we have just discussed. For *bukama* means more than we mean by "kingship"; it also has strong implications of proprietorship and even personal ownership. And *bulemi* means a good deal more than merely "government." It is associated with the verb *kulema,* one of the commonest verbs in the language, and its primary meaning is "to rule," but it has the further strong implication of a thing's being difficult and burdensome. Thus Nyoro say "the king rules his people," "a master rules his servants," and so on, but they also say of a task or problem—or even of a person—which has proved intractable, "it has ruled me" (*kindemere*), meaning that it has been too difficult to cope with. The idea of being overcome, subordinated to something more powerful than oneself, is an essential part of the meaning of the term. In Chapters 3 and 4 we shall be concerned with the political side of Nyoro social life.

To this field of sometimes oppressive political activity Nyoro oppose the sphere of the community—the intimate, face-to-face relationships which subsist between fellow villagers, neighbors, and kinsmen who see each other constantly and who share the same kind of social background, interests, and values. At this community level, everybody knows everybody else, and there is a kind of corporateness which makes the community conscious of itself as against other communities and, especially, as against the superimposed govern-mental system. The Nyoro term *kyaro* ("a place where people stay") refers to the territorial aspect of the community; the rights and obligations which it entails are implied in the terms for clanship, consanguinity, and, in particular, neighborhood. In Chapters 5 and 6, and in the greater part of Chapter 7, we shall be dealing with relationships characteristic of the local community. We shall find that Nyoro themselves are well aware of the conflicts which may arise between community values and those of the state, with its implication of subjection and subordination to a superior authority.

This leads to the second and associated notion—in fact an aspect of the notion just discussed—which I found to be most strikingly characteristic of Nyoro culture: the idea of superordination and subordination. It is remarkable that in Bunyoro this idea of "ruling" is not restricted to the political sphere (though of course it is especially characteristic of this sphere); it pervades the whole field of social relations. Almost all institutionalized social relationships in Bunyoro have an inegalitarian, hierarchical aspect; the notion that people occupy different categories, and that these are almost always unequal, is ubiqui-tous. Thus Nyoro often speak of fathers as being superior to and ruling their children, fathers-in-law as ruling their daughters' husbands, husbands their wives, "sisters' sons" their "mothers' brothers," and so on. Through the whole field of social relations, those of community as well as those of the state, we find this notion of ruling, of exercising authority over someone. In some African societies the homely idiom of kinship is extended even into the field of political relations; in Bunyoro the tendency is in the reverse direction: here the idiom of government, of ruling, is extended from the political into the community and even into the domestic sphere. Such a state of affairs is consistent with the centralized, "feudal" structure of Bunyoro, in which all authority, right down to the base of the pyramid, is thought of as being at least ideally derived from and validated by the Mukama.

2

Myth and History

Myth

WHAT INTERESTS US most about myths is the way in which they may express attitudes and beliefs current at the present time. Mythologies always embody systems of values, judgments about what is considered good and proper by the people who have the myth. Especially, myth tends to sustain some system of authority, and the distinctions of power and status which this implies. Thus Nyoro myths tend to validate the kinds of social and political stratification which I have said are characteristic of the culture, and to support the kingship around which the traditional political system revolved. In Malinowski's phrase, Nyoro legend provides a "mythical charter" for the social and political order.

For Nyoro, human history begins with a first family, whose head is sometimes called Kintu, "the created thing." There are three children in this family, all boys. At first these are not distinguished from one another by name; all are called "Kana," which means "little child." This is of course confusing, and Kintu asks God if they may be given separate names. God agrees, and the boys are submitted to two tests. First, six things are placed on a path by which the boys will pass. These are an ox's head, a cowhide thong, a bundle of cooked millet and potatoes, a grass head-ring (for carrying loads on the head), an axe, and a knife. When the boys come upon these things, the eldest at once picks up the bundle of food and starts to eat. What he cannot eat he carries away, using the head-ring for this purpose. He also takes the axe and the knife. The second son takes the leather thong, and the youngest takes the ox's head, which is all that is left. In the next test the boys have to sit on the ground in the evening, with their legs stretched out, each holding on his lap a wooden milk-pot full of milk. They are told that they must hold their pots safely until morning. At midnight the youngest boy begins to nod, and he spills a little of his milk. He wakes up with a start, and begs his brothers

11

for some of theirs. Each gives him a little, so that his pot is full again. Just before dawn the eldest brother suddenly spills all his milk. He, too, asks his brothers to help fill his pot from theirs, but they refuse, saying that it would take too much of their milk to fill his empty pot. In the morning their father finds the youngest son's pot full, the second son's nearly full, and the eldest's quite empty.

He gives his decision, and names the three boys. The eldest, and his descendants after him, is always to be a servant and a cultivator, and to carry loads for his younger brothers, and their descendants. For he chose the millet and potatoes, peasants' food, and he lost all the milk entrusted to him, so showing himself unfit to have anything to do with cattle. Thus he was named "Kairu," which means little Iru or peasant. The second son and his descendants would have the respected status of cattlemen. For he had chosen the leather thong for tying cattle, and he had spilt none of his milk, only providing some for his younger brother. So he was called "Kahuma," little cowherd or Huma, and ever since the cattle-herding people of this part of the interlacustrine region have been called Huma or Hima. But the third and youngest son would be his father's heir, for he had taken the ox's head, a sign that he would be at the head of all men, and he alone had a full bowl of milk when morning came, because of the help given him by his brothers. So he was named "Kakama," little Mukama or ruler. He and his descendants became the kings of Bunyoro, or Kitara, as the country was then called. When the three brothers had been named, their father told the two elder that they should never leave their young brother, but should stay with him and serve him always. And he told Kakama to rule wisely and well.

This myth explains and justifies the traditional division of Nyoro society into distinct social categories based on descent. At the beginning, people were undifferentiated—this is symbolized by the three boys having no separate names or identities—but this was confusing, and the only orderly solution was to grade them in three hierarchically ordered categories. It is true that in Bunyoro the distinction between Hima and Iru is of decreasing social importance, but the distinctions of status implied by the myth and especially the differential allocation of authority are still strongly marked in social life. What is validated is basically the "givenness" of differences of status and authority based on birth and, in general, the preeminence of ascribed status over personal achievement. Subordinates may find subordination less irksome, and superordinates may rule more calmly and confidently, when everyone acknowledges the difference between them and the divine origin of that difference.

Many stories, all of which point a moral, are told of the very first kings, Kakama's earliest descendants. The following is one of the best known. King Isaza came to the throne as a very young man; he was disrespectful toward the elders whom his father had left to advise him, and he drove them away from the palace, replacing them by gay youngsters with whom he used to go hunting, which was his favorite pastime. One day he killed a zebra, and he was so pleased with its gaily striped hide that he determined to dress himself in it at once. So his young companions sewed the skin on him. But as the day wore on, the hot sun dried the skin, and it quickly shrank and began to squeeze Isaza until he was nearly dead. He begged his friends for help, but they just laughed at him and did nothing. When he had driven the old men away, two had stayed nearby, and now Isaza sent to them for help. First they refused, but after a while they relented, and told Isaza's young men to throw the king into a pond. They did so, and the moisture loosened the hide so that it could be removed. Isaza was so grateful to the old men that he called them all back to the palace, gave them a feast and reinstated them. At the same time he reprimanded his young associates, telling them that they should always respect the old.

This Nyoro "cautionary tale" points the familiar moral that a person in authority neglects at his peril the advice of those older and wiser than he, and that old men are likely to be better informed than callow youths. But it also stresses another important feature of Nyoro ideas about authority— namely, that it is not inappropriate for young persons to have power. It will be remembered that in the previous myth it was the youngest son, not the eldest, who succeeded to his father's authority; in fact, succession by the youngest, or a younger, son is a characteristic feature of Nyoro inheritance. The role of the older brother is to act as guardian until the heir is old enough to assume full authority. Nyoro say that a first son should not inherit; we shall see that the Mukama may not be succeeded by his eldest son. But the Isaza myth also stresses the wisdom of the old, and the respect due to them. Age is a qualification for advisory, not executive, authority; it is right that the aged should be spared the arduousness of decision making, but right that they should guide and advise those in power. The legend of Isaza and the zebra skin is a popular one, for it expresses values important to Nyoro and which we shall meet again.

It is important also to examine the cycle of dynastic myths which merge into traditional history and link up (if the series be regarded chronologically) with the "real" history which we shall go on to consider. Nyoro believe that there have been three royal dynasties; first, the shadowy Tembuzi, of whom Kakama was the first and Isaza the last; second, the Chwezi, part-legendary hero-gods whose marvelous exploits are still spoken of; and third, the Bito, the line to which the present king belongs. We shall see that part of the significance of the myths which we now discuss lies in the way in which they link these three dynasties together into a single line of descent, so creating an unbroken chain between the present ruler and the very first king of Bunyoro.

The story is rich in descriptive detail, but here we can only give an outline account. It begins by telling how the king of the world of ghosts, called Nyamiyonga, sent a message to king Isaza (whose hunting exploit has just been recounted) asking him to enter into a blood pact with him. Isaza's councilors advised against this, so Isaza had the pact made on Nyamiyonga's behalf with his chief minister, a commoner called Bukuku. When Nyamiyonga discovered that he had been united in the blood pact with an Iru or commoner, he was angry, and he determined to get Isaza into his power. So he sent his beautiful daughter Nyamata to Isaza's court, where she so attracted the king that he married her, not knowing who she was. But he resisted all her efforts to persuade him to visit her home, for he could not bear to be parted from his cattle, which he loved more than anything else. So Nyamiyonga thought of another plan. He caused two of his most handsome cattle to be discovered near Isaza's kraal, and these were taken to the king, who soon loved them most of all his herd. One day they disappeared, and the distracted Mukama went in search of them, leaving Bukuku to rule the kingdom in his absence. After much wandering, Isaza arrived in the country of ghosts, where he found his two cattle and also his wife Nyamata, who had gone home some time previously to bear him a child. Nyamiyonga welcomed the Nyoro king, but he had not forgiven him, and he never allowed him to return to the world of men.

In due course Nyamata's child was born and was named Isimbwa. When Isimbwa grew up he married in the world of ghosts and had a son called Kyomya, of whom we shall hear more later. Isimbwa, unlike his father, could visit the world of living men, and on a hunting expedition he came to the capital where Bukuku still reigned in Isaza's place. Bukuku was unpopular because he was a commoner and had no real right to rule, but there was no one else to do so. He had a daughter called Nyinamwiru, and at Nyinamwiru's birth diviners had told Bukuku that he would have reason to fear any child that she might bear. So he kept her in a special enclosure which could only be entered through his own well-guarded palace. When Isimbwa reached Bukuku's capital he was intrigued by this state of affairs, and after making clandestine advances to Nyinamwiru through her maid, he managed to climb into her enclosure and, unknown to Bukuku, he stayed there for three months. He then left the kingdom and was not seen again for many years.

After a time Nyinamwiru bore a son, to the consternation of Bukuku, who gave orders for the child to be drowned. So the baby was thrown in a river, but by chance its umbilical cord caught in a bush, and the child was discovered by a potter, Rubumbi, who took it home and brought it up as a member of his family. He knew that it was Nyinamwiru's child, and he told her that it was safe. Bukuku, of course, believed it to be dead. The boy grew up strong and spirited, and was constantly in trouble with Bukuku's herdsmen, for when the king's cattle were being watered he would drive them away, so that he could water Rubumbi's cattle first. This angered Bukuku, who one day came to the drinking trough himself to punish the unruly potter's son. But before Bukuku's men could carry out his orders to seize and beat him, he rushed round to the back of Bukuku's royal stool and stabbed him mortally with his spear. He then sat down on the king's stool. The herdsmen were aghast, and ran at once to tell Nyinamwiru what had happened. The story tells that she was both glad and sorry; glad because her son had taken the throne, sorry because of her father's death. So Ndahura, which is what the young man was called, came to his grandfather Isaza's throne, and he is reckoned as the first of the Chwezi kings.

There were only three—some say two—Chwezi kings; Ndahura, his half-brother Mulindwa, and his son Wamara. Many wonderful things are told of their wisdom and achievements, but during Wamara's reign things began to go badly for them. So they called their diviners and an ox was cut open so that its entrails could be examined. The diviners were astonished to find no trace of the intestines, and they did not know what to say. At that moment a stranger from north of the Nile appeared, and said that he was a diviner and would solve the riddle for them. But first he insisted (wisely, as it turned out) on making a blood pact with one of the Chwezi, so that he could be safe from their anger if his findings were unfavorable. Then he took an axe and cut open the head and hooves of the ox. At once the missing intestines fell out of these members, and as they did so a black smut from the fire settled on them, and could not be removed.

The Nilotic diviner then said that the absence of the intestines from their proper place meant that the rule of the Chwezi in Bunyoro was over. Their presence in the hoofs meant that they would wander far away; in the head, that they would, nonetheless, continue to rule over men (a reference to the possession cult, centered on the Chwezi spirits, which will be discussed in Chapter 7). And the black smut meant that the kingdom would be taken over by dark-skinned strangers from the north. So the Chwezi departed from Bunyoro, no one knows whither.

Meantime the diviner went back to his own country in the north, and there he met the sons of Kyomya, who was, it will be remembered, Isimbwa's son by his first wife. Kyomya had married in the country to the north of the Nile, and had settled down there. The diviner told Kyomya's sons that they should go south and take over the abandoned Nyoro kingdom of their Tembuzi grandfathers. There were four brothers altogether: Nyarwa, the eldest; the twins Rukidi Mpuga and Kato Kimera; and Kiiza, the youngest. They were the first Bito. Nyarwa (as we might expect) did not become a ruler, though some say that he remained as adviser to his second brother Rukidi, who became the first Bito king of Bunyoro. Kato was allotted Buganda, then a dependency of the great Nyoro empire (Ganda, of course, have a rather different version of these events), and Kiiza was given a part of what is now Busoga, a country many miles to the east of present-day Bunyoro.

When the Bito first arrived in Bunyoro, they seemed strange and uncouth to the inhabitants. It is said that half of Rukidi's body was black and half white, a reference to his mixed descent. They had to be instructed in the manners appropriate to rulers; at first, they were ignorant of such important matters as cattle keeping and milk drinking. But gradually Rukidi assumed the values and manners proper to the heir of the pastoral rulers of the earlier dynasties. So began the reign of the powerful Bito dynasty, which has lasted up to the present.

This series of myths establishes a genealogical link between the three recognized dynasties of Nyoro rulers. Having noted the importance in Bunyoro of hereditarily determined status, we can see that a major function is served by the genealogical linking of the present ruling line with the wonderful Chwezi, whose exploits are still talked of throughout the region, and, through them, with the even more remote Tembuzi and so with the very beginnings of human existence. The connection enables the present ruling line to claim descent of an honor and antiquity not exceeded even by that of the pastoral Huma (who are said in some contexts to look down upon the Bito as "commoners"). The marking off of the ruling Bito from all other Nyoro contributes to their unity and exclusiveness, and so lends validity to their claims to special respect, prestige, and authority. And not only the rulers, but all Nyoro, share in the glory of their ruling line and the wonderful feats of its progenitors. The exploits and conquests of Isaza and the Chwezi rulers are known to every Nyoro. When people think of themselves, as Nyoro sometimes do (for reasons which will become plain later), as being in decline, there may be compensation in the thought of past in default of present greatness. And we may suppose that historically the genealogical link was important for the immigrant Bito, who lacked the prestige of the already existing Huma aristocracy, and needed the enhancement of status which this "genealogical charter" provided. So the main social function of Nyoro mythical history is the establishment of Bito credentials to govern, by emphasizing the distinction and antiquity of their genealogical antecedents.

According to the myth, the present Mukama is descended in an unbroken patrilineal line[1] from the very beginning of things, and it may well be asked (as indeed it has been) why in this case there are said to have been three dynasties in Nyoro history, and not only one. But the question implies a too literal interpretation of the myth. The fact is that for Nyoro there *are* three dynasties, and whatever the truth about their real relationship to one another, if any (or even, in the case of the earlier ones, their very existence), Nyoro believe them to have been three quite different kinds of people. In other contexts the Chwezi are spoken of as a strange and wonderful people who came from far away, took over the kingdom from the Tembuzi, remained in the country for a generation or two, and then mysteriously disappeared. There is linguistic and other evidence to support the view that the Bito are of quite different racial and cultural stock from the people whose country and kingship they took over. The myth is not to be understood as an attempt to reconstruct a history that has been lost forever; it is rather to be seen as providing a genealogical charter for a structure of authority whose existence is contemporaneous with the myth itself.

History

The story of the Bito dynasty, from the time of its first king, Rukidi, until the arrival of the Europeans in the middle of the nineteenth century, spans perhaps eighteen generations. Many stories are told of its kings, and they become more detailed and circumstantial as we approach historical times. Myth, chronologically regarded, begins to merge into history. Here we can only indicate general trends. The traditional history of the Bito dynasty falls

---

[1] *Patrilineal* descent is reckoned exclusively through males—that is, through the father, the father's father, and so on.

into two parts. During the first period, up to the time of the seventeenth Bito king, the great empire believed to have been inherited from the Chwezi was maintained in much of its former greatness. The fourth Bito Mukama fought with the Ganda, who had by now asserted their independence, and killed their king. Other Bito kings are said to have fought successful wars as far away as the borders of Zande country in the Congo, and in Ruanda and Ankole, the latter of which is said to have been a part of the Nyoro empire until about the end of this period. There were constant wars against the small but aggressive Ganda kingdom. At all periods there were numerous revolts, but these were usually successfully quelled. The second period, from the reign of the seventeenth Mukama until historical times, is marked by a gradual decline in Nyoro fortunes, brought about both by successful revolts in outlying areas and by annexations by the Ganda, whose expanding state now began to acquire the wider political dominance which it holds at the present time. The decline was not continuous, for strong kings sometimes temporarily reversed it; but losses tended to exceed gains, and when the historical period begins, Bunyoro, though still a substantial and powerful kingdom, was no longer comparable in size or importance to the ancient Kitara empire. Thus by the reign of the present king's great-great-grandfather, the one-time province of Toro had asserted its independence (though it needed European support to maintain it), Ankole had long since become a separate kingdom, Buganda had gained much Nyoro territory in the east, and we hear no more of successful campaigns in far-away regions like Ruanda and the Zande country. But Bunyoro was still very much a power to be reckoned with; the final blow to its former greatness was struck not by the Ganda, or at least not by them alone, but by the Europeans.

The history of Bunyoro since the 1860's is essentially a history of European-Nyoro relations. There might indeed be said to be two different histories of these relations—a European one and a Nyoro one—and it would be possible and perhaps instructive to give these as two separate accounts. For they exemplify a situation, only too familiar in relations between peoples of different cultures (especially when one is subordinated to the other), in which the same events are so differently regarded by different people that misunderstanding is added to misunderstanding, and in the end serious conflict arises. This is a practical aspect of the problem of communication which was considered in the last chapter. But such a dual treatment of our material would be tedious and repetitious, so for reasons of space and for simplicity of presentation I give a single account, indicating important points of difference or misunderstanding as they occur. The story could fill a book by itself, so here I can record only the most important events.

The first Europeans to visit Bunyoro were the explorers Speke and Grant. When they arrived, in 1862, Mukama Kamurasi (the present king's grandfather) was at the head of a kingdom which was very much larger than present-day Bunyoro. It included much of what is now Buganda, parts of the present Toro and Ankole districts, and it extended some distance north and east of the Nile and west of Lake Albert. But although it seems that all these regions acknowledged the suzerainty of the Nyoro king, it would be a mistake to picture the whole as an orderly and well-administered political unit. There were frequent revolts, sometimes led by dissident "princes," members of the royal Bito clan (the first establishment of Toro as a separate kingdom was the result of such a successful rebellion), and there were constant wars with Buganda, then rapidly increasing in size and power.

Speke and Grant came straight from the Ganda court to Kamurasi's capital, and they stayed there for two months before going north to the Sudan. They described the Mukama as "not unkindly," and as "of a mild disposition compared with Mutesa" (the Ganda king). But they found him suspicious, and they were irritated by his constant demands for gifts and for armed help against his cousin Ruyonga, who was in revolt in the north of the kingdom. Nevertheless they left the country safely, hoping that they had succeeded in laying the foundations of future good relations between Europeans and the Nyoro kingdom. Unfortunately their confidence was misplaced; certainly it was not shared by Nyoro. The Europeans had come straight from the hostile Ganda king, accompanied by a Ganda escort, and furthermore they did not come together but separately, like enemies preparing an attack. And the Ganda, then (as later) anxious to foment trouble between Nyoro and Europeans, in order both to discomfit their traditional enemies and to keep European favor and its concomitant advantages for themselves, spread stories among the Nyoro that the Europeans were cannibals, and given to the most terrible deeds. Ridiculous though these tales seemed to Speke and Grant, they naturally seemed less so to Kamurasi and his advisers, who had never seen Europeans before. Nevertheless the visitors were treated hospitably, and given ample food and beer. And if Kamurasi was sometimes exigent in his demands for gifts and assistance, this was natural enough when these alarming but ostensibly well-disposed strangers were so rich in powerful firearms and other unfamiliar and desirable things.

A little over a year later the explorer Samuel Baker and his intrepid wife arrived from the north, having met Speke and Grant on their way. They spent an uncomfortable year in the country, in the course of which they discovered and named Lake Albert (of course it already had a name, "Mwitanzige," or "the killer of locusts," but such considerations as this rarely inhibited the nomenclatural proclivities of Victorian explorers). Baker and his wife possessed amazing hardihood and courage, but he was a blunt and tactless man, and his relations with Kamurasi were continuously strained. He wrote bitterly about him in his book about this expedition, and accused him of treachery, cowardice, and greed. He and his wife left the country safely, however, and when we consider the circumstances of their arrival this may be thought remarkable enough.

These circumstances included the fact that shortly after Speke's and Grant's departure in the previous year a party of Sudanese had arrived from the north claiming to be these Europeans' greatest friends. After they had been hospitably received on this account they suddenly turned on their hosts and, in collusion with Kamurasi's enemy Ruyonga, killed about three hundred of them. Of course this was not the Europeans' fault, but it is not surprising that Kamurasi and his people were subsequently more than a little suspicious of strangers, especially white ones. Another factor which determined Nyoro reactions to the Bakers' visit was the latters' close association with one of the several Sudanese slaving gangs which were at this time operating, with quite appalling savagery, in what is now the southern Sudan and northern Uganda. These large armed gangs, whose guns gave them the advantage over any local tribe, used to ally themselves with one tribal ruler against another, taking as reward for their aid a rich booty of slaves, ivory, and cattle from the defeated side. Often they would then turn on their allies and add their women and cattle to their spoil. These raiders caused vast destruction and misery; whole regions were depopulated, for many of those who were not carried off or killed died from famine or disease consequent to the destruction of their homes, crops, and cattle. A man is known by the company he keeps, and even though Baker did his best to avoid participation in his companions' raids and intrigues, it was hardly surprising that the Mukama and his people regarded him with deep suspicion.

Unfortunately he did little to counteract this inevitable impression. He even went so far as to threaten Kamurasi with severe reprisals from these very raiders if he did not do what he wanted. Kamurasi once complained to Baker about the bad behavior of one of the latter's Sudanese associates, who had insulted him publicly and threatened him with a gun. Kamurasi told Baker that had the Sudanese not been one of Baker's companions he would have had him and his men killed. Baker, instead of apologizing for his associate's offensive behavior, or even undertaking to look into the matter, advised Kamurasi "not to talk too big, as . . . he might imagine the results that would occur should he even hint at hostility, as the large parties of Ibrahim and the men of Mohamed Wat-el-Mek [two of Baker's Sudanese associates] would immediately unite and destroy both him and his country." Baker reports that "the gallant Kamurasi turned almost green at the bare suggestion of this possibility." (See Baker 1867.) This incident provides a good example of Baker's manner of dealing with the Nyoro king, and helps to explain the suspicion with which Kamurasi and his chiefs regarded him.

The Bakers left Bunyoro in 1864, and returned eight years later, Sir Samuel Baker (as he now was) having been appointed governor-general of the Egyptian province of Equatoria, in which Bunyoro was supposed to be included. He found that Kamurasi had died two years earlier, and had been succeeded by his son Kabarega. During this visit, which only lasted for a few months, there was constant friction between Baker and Kabarega, ending in open conflict shortly after Baker had formally proclaimed the annexation of Bunyoro to Egypt, in the presence of the Mukama and his chiefs. Baker claims that he had first obtained Kabarega's consent to the annexation, but Nyoro deny this. A few days later there was a fight, after the king had (according to Baker) sent poisoned beer to the European and his men, from the fatal effects of which they were only saved by the prompt administration of emetics. Shortly after, Baker states, he and his men were treacherously attacked, and after an affray in which he had to defend himself with a machine gun, he was forced to retreat northwards to the Nile. Here he proclaimed the now aging rebel Ruyonga as the official representative of the Egyptian government in Bunyoro, authorizing him to rule, on Egypt's behalf, in Kabarega's place. This coup had little effect on the existing political situation and of course none at all on Kabarega's authority, though no doubt it relieved Baker's feelings. Unfortunately it did have some historical repercussions.

Naturally the Nyoro version of these events differs considerably from Baker's. I have spoken of the ravages of the slave trade, and in the interval since Baker's first visit these had extended into northern Bunyoro. The slavers were known to come from Khartoum, which most Nyoro did not clearly distinguish from Egypt, so Baker could not have expected to be received with open arms when he returned as a representative of that country. Further, Baker's Sudanese followers inflicted revolting cruelties and abuses on the people everywhere they went. Nor was Baker's hurried annexation of the country just before he fled from it calculated to increase Nyoro confidence in European intentions. Nyoro say that Kabarega and his chiefs were surprised and indignant at Baker's action. They also say that the beer sent to Baker and his men was not poisoned but just particularly strong, and that they drank too much of it. In the fracas which followed these events, they say, Baker mowed down large numbers of Nyoro with a Maxim gun, set fire to the king's enclosure and all the neighboring villages, and departed.

We cannot now know the truth about these events, nor is it our present concern to conjecture about it, still less to allocate praise or blame to either party. My present point is that, whatever actually happened, there subsequently existed two quite different histories of it, one held by Nyoro, the other incorporated into the European record. Certainly some efforts were afterwards made to modify the latter; Emin Pasha, writing five years later, reported that he received in Bunyoro an account of Baker's visit very different from that given by Baker, and many years afterwards the missionary-anthropologist Roscoe, who visited Bunyoro in 1920, also heard the Nyoro version, and noted the serious effects of the affair on Kabarega's attitude to Europeans. But by this time the damage had long since been done; already in the 1870's two different and conflicting versions of Bunyoro's first relations with Europeans had, in Collingwood's phrase, "incapsulated" themselves in the unfolding series of events, and the basis had been laid for further misunderstanding and hostility.

Baker was succeeded as governor of Equatoria by the famous soldier Colonel Gordon, whose attitude to Kabarega and the Nyoro was naturally influenced by Baker's reports. He completely ignored the Nyoro king, dealing instead with Baker's puppet Ruyonga. Gordon's main concern was to stamp out the slave trade, and to do this he established fortified posts in northern Bunyoro and elsewhere, which he staffed with Sudanese and Egyptian soldiers, without, of course, consulting Kabarega first. The Nyoro king and his people were bound to consider this provocative, especially as the occupying garrisons were scarcely less of a menace to the local populations than the slavers themselves. Nevertheless, Nyoro say, Kabarega did not attack these forts, for he did not wish to start fighting the Europeans. Gordon was succeeded in 1878 by the curious and complex German doctor known as Emin Pasha, who unlike his predecessors (and most of his successors) was a trained scientist and scholar as well as an administrator and an explorer. Alone among these early Europeans Emin got on well with Kabarega, and spoke highly, even warmly, of his character and intelligence. Emin's administration lasted much longer than either of his predecessors', and seems to have been successful until the repercussions of the Mahdi revolt in the Sudan in 1884 led to his isolation and to the final breakdown of his administration. Even though Emin realized that Kabarega never really trusted him or any European, his tact and good sense enabled relations to be maintained on a friendly enough basis for several years. But with Emin's reluctant departure with Stanley in 1889 this relatively satisfactory state of affairs came to an end; Kabarega began a new series of raids into Buganda and Toro, and from this time onwards relations between Europeans and the Nyoro king were hostile.

In 1890 Captain Lugard arrived in Uganda as a representative of the British East Africa Company, within whose sphere of influence Buganda and the surrounding regions, including Bunyoro, now fell. Unlike Baker, Gordon, and Emin, he approached Bunyoro from the east, through Buganda, and not from the north, and there is evidence that the Kabaka of Buganda and his advisers made the most of their opportunity to prejudice Lugard against the western kingdom. Lugard relied on Baker's account of Kabarega's character, and it is plain from his own writings that he never even considered the possibility of negotiating with the Nyoro king. Shortly after his arrival in Uganda he decided to collect and reenlist the Sudanese soldiers who were supposed to have remained in the region of Lake Albert after Emin's departure, and to use them to maintain order in Buganda, which was then in a very disturbed condition. On his way there he confirmed a young man called Kasagama, whom he had found as a fugitive in Buganda, as king of Toro, a region which had formerly been part of Bunyoro, but which had revolted a generation or two earlier, and which Kabarega had recently been attempting to regain. This inevitably involved some brushes with Kabarega's warriors. Lugard eventually collected from the neighborhood of Lake Albert about six hundred Sudanese troops, together with their now numerous camp followers and dependants, and he used some of these to garrison a chain of forts which he established across northern Toro, with the object of protecting the new king and his people from Kabarega's attacks. These undisciplined troops soon started to lay waste the country around the forts, which in turn led to more reprisals by Kabarega's men. These forays intensified Lugard's conviction that there could be no peaceful settlement with Kabarega. He acknowledges that envoys came to him from Bunyoro to sue for peace, but he refused to negotiate with them, on the ground that Kabarega was so implacably opposed to Europeans that there would be little point in doing so. He was determined to conquer Bunyoro by force of arms, and serious preparations were now made for a campaign.

So in 1893, after an ultimatum had been issued to Kabarega calling for guarantees for his future good conduct and a substantial indemnity for his past misdeeds, to which apparently no reply was received, a force of nearly 15,000 men, over 14,000 of whom were Ganda, invaded Bunyoro under European leadership. They quickly overran the country, but Kabarega, though constantly harried by the invaders, carried on in retreat a protracted guerrilla warfare, sometimes north and sometimes south of the Nile. In the following year Kabarega's forces sustained some major defeats, but he was still in the field, and in 1895 an even more enormous army was sent against him, consisting of six companies of Sudanese with two Hotchkiss and three Maxim guns, and twenty thousand Ganda. In 1896 the commander of these forces reported that Kabarega had been driven from his country and many hundreds of cattle captured. But although the traditional Nyoro state had been reduced to chaos and the population was undergoing great hardships, the elusive Kabarega still held out with a few followers north of the Nile. Not until 1899 was he finally captured, after being severely wounded in the final engagement. He was exiled to the Seychelles islands, but was allowed to return in 1923, by which time he was an old man. He died on the way, without seeing Bunyoro again.

Nyoro think that the long military campaign against Kabarega was unjustified, and that their Mukama was a good deal less intransigent than he was said to be. They believe that Lugard was misled by the Ganda, and that Kabarega would have been willing to come to terms if he had been allowed to do so. They point out that his overtures were always repulsed, or else huge indemnities were asked, as though he were doing wrong in occupying and defending his own country. Throughout the campaign, Nyoro say, the king carefully avoided directly attacking the Europeans. He did what a king should do; he fought a defensive war, in the face of huge odds, against invasion. Nyoro believe that the British attitude toward their country was due largely to Ganda misrepresentation, and indeed the Ganda did profit handsomely by the downfall of their old enemy.

At the end of the nineteenth century, Bunyoro was thus in very poor shape. The country was largely depopulated by war, famine, and disease. It was regarded as conquered territory, and its administration was for the most part in the hands of Ganda chiefs, who were sent there to teach the Nyoro how to govern themselves. With their king captured and exiled, their country devastated, disease and famine on all sides, and their hereditary enemies the Ganda lording it over them, Bunyoro's downfall was complete. In 1900 Sir Harry Johnston concluded the famous Uganda Agreement with the three regents of Buganda. As well as laying down the principles which should govern political relations between Buganda and the Protectorate government, this agreement defined the territorial boundaries of the Ganda kingdom. Within these it included some large and populous areas which were, as everybody (including Johnston) knew, part of Bunyoro. Thus at a stroke the Nyoro were punished for their resistance and the Ganda rewarded for their assistance to the British campaign. As a result almost 40 percent of the Nyoro people have lived in Ganda territory and been subject to Ganda chiefs for the past half-century, a state of affairs which the Mukama of Bunyoro and his people still deeply resent, especially as the graves of almost all of the former kings of Bunyoro, which are national monuments of great importance, lie in this alienated area. The Uganda Agreement also provided that many chiefs and other important people in Buganda should receive what amounted to freehold rights over large areas of land. It was afterwards recognized that this provision was based on a misconception. But by then the Agreement had been made and it was too late to alter things; the notion of private ownership in land had been irrevocably introduced. The Government was determined not to repeat what it believed to have been an error, and despite repeated claims by the king of Bunyoro and his chiefs (who regarded this as another instance of discrimination) no similar grants of land were made in Bunyoro.

A settled civil administration began to be established in Bunyoro soon after 1900, and the past half-century has shown steady political and economic advance. By the end of World War I almost all the Ganda chiefs had been replaced by Nyoro, and in 1933 the Bunyoro Agreement provided the kingdom with a political status analagous to, though not quite as favorable as, that enjoyed by Buganda. But Nyoro think that even during the past fifty years they have suffered from disabilities not shared by the neighboring kingdoms. The tenure of most of Bunyoro's important chiefships by Ganda in the early years of the century rankled, and in 1906 a number of Nyoro chiefs and people demonstrated in protest. Some chiefs were sentenced to terms of imprisonment or exile in consequence. During the first decade of this century, also, famine continued to afflict Bunyoro. It is said that in the 1920's the remnants of Bunyoro's herds of cattle, already decimated by war and disease, succumbed in large numbers to anti-rinderpest inoculations carried out by the Government. The Government's intention, of course, was to help, not to injure, the Nyoro, but many people still believe that these deaths were the result of a policy designed to keep Nyoro in a properly humble and submissive state.

Even European missionary activity has been regarded as being directed to the same end, and some pagan Nyoro still so regard it. The old religious cult, centering on spirit possession, is still strong, and one of its most important aims is the ensuring of fertility. Many other magical rites are directed to the same purpose, and to the health and prosperity of their practitioners. All these practices have been rigorously suppressed both by missions and by the Government, and Nyoro have told me that this is because the Europeans do not really want Nyoro to increase in numbers, health, or prosperity. Such beliefs are by no means absurd to semiliterate Africans with no first-hand knowledge of Europeans. Certainly the rigor with which indigenous Nyoro religious and magical cults have been suppressed is unusual in an African dependency; even the missionary anthropologist Roscoe criticized this repressive policy, the chief effect of which has been to drive these practices underground.

To bring this history quite up to date, reference would have to be made to Bunyoro's increased economic prosperity, and to the several constitutional advances which have been made in recent years, providing for the increased devolution of authority on to the Mukama and his chiefs and, latterly, on to the people themselves, through popular representation on the chiefs' councils.

Some of these matters have already been touched on; others will be considered when we discuss the contemporary political system in the next two chapters. Thus far I have attempted to bring to life Nyoro ideas about their own past, and to do this I have had to review the history of European-Nyoro relations. It should, perhaps, be reaffirmed that it is no part of the social anthropologist's task to say what should or should not be, or have been, done: he knows that people are bound to act within the broad lines that their culture prescribes, and that, for example, the ideas and standards of a Victorian soldier or explorer are bound to differ vastly from those of a tribal African king, and even very considerably from our own. So he will not make the elementary mistake of condemning either party for failing to act in accordance with contemporary standards of practical morality and psychological "know-how." But there is no doubt that Bunyoro has been unlucky in some of her relationships with Europeans, and that some of her grievances are real ones. Only when we have understood this can we understand how contemporary Nyoro think about themselves and about Europeans, and how Europeans think about Nyoro. It is because Nyoro are historians, not because we are, that this historical section has had to be included; a book about Bunyoro which neglected its history would be like *Hamlet,* if not without the Prince of Denmark, at least without his father's ghost.

3

The King

Rituals of Kingship

SOMETHING has already been said of the kingship, and in the last chapter we followed the fortunes of the most famous of Nyoro kings, the redoubtable Kabarega. We now examine the Nyoro monarchy first as the symbol of Nyoro nationhood, the focus of Nyoro ideas about political authority, and second, as the center of the network of social relations which is what we mean when we talk about the political system. Therefore in the first part of this chapter I consider the ways in which the kingship is traditionally regarded; this will entail a discussion of its ritual character. In the second part I discuss the king's actual relationships with the different kinds of people who make up Nyoro society; this will enable us to determine his position in the social structure. Throughout, our main interest is in the present-day situation. But we cannot understand this unless we understand the traditional elements which still persist. What I describe is still in important respects a traditional African monarchy, but it has been much modified by European influence, and in the course of my account I shall take note of these modifications. This will reflect the manner in which these modifications present themselves to the field anthropologist, indeed to thoughtful Nyoro themselves; that is, as impacting at various points and in various ways on a traditional political organization.

We have seen how myth and traditional history validate the Mukama's claim to special distinction. He and his Bito kinsmen are thought of (and think of themselves) as quite different from ordinary people. Unlike some African rulers, Nyoro kings are not thought of as kin with the people they rule; they are not "fathers" of their people, but rulers of their people. Where the distinction between those born to rule and those born to be ruled is as sharply made as it is in Bunyoro, the intimacy of a blood tie (which in fact always exists through the female line, since kings' mothers come from non-Bito

25

clans) between these two quite different kinds of people is unlikely to be asserted, even in metaphor. The Mukama is the traditional ruler of all Nyoro, and in pre-European times all political authority in the state was seen as deriving from him. Nowadays, of course, outside political power is injected into the system at all levels by government officials, missionaries, and others, and nearly everybody knows this. But the Nyoro kingship is still essentially authoritarian. There are African kingdoms in which the king's importance is traditionally ritual rather than political; in Bunyoro this is not so. Though his power was not absolute, the Mukama was essentially a ruler. He is, indeed, surrounded by ritual, but this ritual makes sense only when it is seen as a symbolic expression of the king's political preeminence and power. A look at some of this ritual will make this point clear.

Broadly, Nyoro royal ritual falls into three categories. First, there are rites which express the ways in which Nyoro think about the kingship itself. Second, there is the ritual associated with the king's accession to and retention of authority, and his relinquishing of it at death. And third, there are those rites which are concerned with the ways in which the king may delegate his authority.

The rituals in the first category are mostly concerned with the Mukama in his aspect as "divine king," which means, for Nyoro, that he is mystically identified with the whole country of which he is the head. This means that the king must keep physically healthy; if he does not, the country and people as a whole will suffer. Formerly, a person, or even an ox, who was sick had to be removed at once from the royal enclosure, in case the king's health should be affected. The king had to avoid all contact with death; when I asked why the present Mukama did not attend his mother's funeral in 1953, I was told that it was because of this rule. In pre-European times, if the Mukama himself fell sick the matter was kept strictly secret. It is said that if his illness were serious, if he suffered any physical incapacity or mutilation, or if he grew too old and feeble to carry out his duties properly, he would either kill himself by taking poison or be killed by one of his wives. This was, of course, because any imperfection or weakness in the king was thought to involve a corresponding danger to the kingdom. We do not know for sure whether any kings ever were killed in this way, but the important thing is that it is thought that they were. This shows us how Nyoro traditionally thought about their country and their kingship.

As well as maintaining physical health, the Mukama had to keep himself in a good ritual or spiritual condition. This imposed on him certain ceremonial acts and avoidances. He was not allowed to eat certain kinds of food which were said to be of low status, such as sweet potatoes, cassava, and certain other vegetables. His numerous attendants also had to keep themselves ritually pure; for instance, his cooks had to abstain from sexual intercourse during and for some days before their periods of service in the palace, which were only for a few days at a time. On ceremonial occasions his special dairy-maids, who had to be virgins, smeared themselves with white clay. This symbolized purity and goodness (for Nyoro, as for many other peoples, whiteness and purity are closely associated—indeed, one word is used for both). The king had to carry out certain rites associated with the royal herd of cattle "for the good of the country." These entailed his presence in the byre at milking time, and his ceremonial drinking of some of the new milk. Other usages also stress the Mukama's difference from and superiority to ordinary people. He has to be spoken to and greeted with special words (he is always addressed, and replies, in the third person singular), and he has a large number of distinctive names and titles. These refer to him as exceeding all men, ruling justly, relieving distress, and so on. Even today the most important officers of his own government kneel to hand him anything or to make a request of him in his own house. There is a special vocabulary referring to the king's person and activities, not used in regard to anyone else. He has extensive regalia, consisting of ancient crowns, drums, spears, stools, and other objects, and all of these have special names and their own custodians. In addition to these regalia keepers there are also a great many palace retainers and household officials of various kinds, most of whom have special names and titles.

The effect of these rituals and ceremonial usages, many of which are still observed, is to stress the Mukama's importance as the head of the state and the source of all political authority within it. By symbolically identifying him with the whole country, they justify his being treated as unique, and show why his physical and spiritual well-being must be sustained, while at the same time they enhance tribal unity by providing a set of symbols acceptable to everybody. But though ritual attaches to the kingship, it would be a mistake to think of the Mukama as a kind of priest, in the sense that he intercedes with a god or gods on behalf of his people. Such intercession is the work of the spirit mediums, initiates into the possession cult which is Bunyoro's traditional religion. The Mukama is not a priest, though he has his priests, just as he is not a rain maker, though he has his rain makers—magical experts who are subject to his discipline and control. In some African countries the real importance of chiefs lies in their magical or religious powers, and if they are secular rulers they are so only in a secondary capacity. In Bunyoro it is otherwise. The Mukama is first and foremost a ruler, and that is how everybody thinks of him.

The second of the broad categories of ritual which I distinguished was that concerned with the acquisition, retention, and relinquishing of kingly power. Nyoro accession ceremonies are lengthy and complex. This is what we should expect. In Bunyoro it is not known who is to be the new king until after the old king is dead. Traditionally the heir to the throne was supposed to be the prince who succeeded in killing whichever of his brothers (and he might have a good many) was his rival for the throne. Thus the successful prince undergoes a great change of status on his accession: formerly he was one of a considerable number of equally eligible princes; now he is king. Nyoro accession ritual marks this assumption of new status in the strongest and most emphatic terms. Both its ritual and political aspects are stressed. The accession ceremonies include washing, shaving, and nail-paring rites, anointment with a special oil and smearing with white chalk, ceremonial milk drinking, and animal sacrifice. In pre-European times, it is said, they included the placing on the throne and the subsequent killing of a "mock king," who would, it was believed, attract to himself the magical dangers which attended the transition to kingship, so protecting the real king. The king's accession to political office is equally stressed. He is handed various objects symbolizing political and military power, such as spears, a bow and arrows, a dagger, and a stick, and he is formally admonished and instructed to rule wisely, to kill his enemies, and to protect his people. His territorial authority is also symbolized in a ceremony in which a man who represents neighboring regions formerly subject to Bunyoro presents him with ivory and some copper bracelets as "tribute." Another rite is the ceremonial acting-out of the settlement of a lawsuit in which one man sues another for debt. This is not really a judicial hearing; it is a symbolic way of impressing on both king and people the important part he is to play as lawgiver and judge. Finally, there is a ceremony in which the king shoots arrows with the bow he has been given toward the four points of the compass, saying as he does so: "Thus I shoot the countries to overcome them." Several of these rites are repeated at "refresher" ceremonies, which used to be held annually.

Accession and "refresher" rites stress the king's attainment to supreme political power equally with his accession to the high ritual status associated with this authority. These themes are also evident in the ritual connected with the Mukama's death. Here what is principally expressed is the continuity of the kingship, even though the king is dead. Traditionally there was an inter-regnum of several months during which two or more of the sons of the dead Mukama might fight for the succession, while civil disorder and confusion prevailed. For some days the king's death was concealed; then a man climbed to the top of one of the houses in the king's enclosure carrying a milk-pot, and hurled this to the ground, shouting "The milk is spilt; the king has been taken away!" As this man descended, he was killed, for such things may not be said. In pre-European times the royal corpse was preserved by disemboweling it and drying it over a slow fire. When a prince had succeeded in winning the kingdom he came and took the late king's jawbone, which had been separated from the corpse and carefully guarded, and had to bury this at a selected place, where a house was built and certain of the late king's regalia preserved under the supervision of a chosen member of the royal Bito clan. The rest of the corpse was buried separately and the grave forgotten; the tombs which are remembered and venerated today are those where the royal jawbones are buried.

The third kind of royal ritual which I distinguished related to the delegation of the Mukama's authority. A ruler—at least in the conditions of a tribal African kingdom—cannot keep all his power to himself, but must give some of it away; this is one of the major limitations on political authority. Thus, like other kings, the Mukama of Bunyoro traditionally had to confer quite a high degree of independent authority on his great chiefs; hence the loose, "feudal" type of organization (involving close interpersonal bonds between king and chiefs) characteristic of traditional Bunyoro.

To delegate political authority to his chiefs was at the same time to confer ritual status upon them. There is a Nyoro word, *Mahano,* denoting a special kind of spiritual power, which is applied to many objects and situations which are strange and awe inspiring. This mysterious potency may be dangerous, calling for the performance of special ritual to preserve or restore normality. It is especially associated with the Mukama; therefore, when he delegates political authority upon his chiefs, he also imparts to them something of his own ritual power. Thus the delegation of political authority is not just an administrative act, it is also a ritual act. The ritual involves, in particular, a ceremony known as "drinking milk" with the Mukama, and it is said that (in the case of important chiefs, at least) the milk formerly was taken from the cows of his special herd. Nowadays, it seems, milk is not used, but roasted coffee berries are handed by the Mukama to the person upon whom he is bestowing authority. The recipient of this favor is then supposed to kiss the Mukama's hand, a ceremony strikingly reminiscent of the kiss of fealty in medieval and later Europe. This expresses the chief's obligation and personal devotion to his sovereign, who has confirmed him in authority over a specific territory and its inhabitants. Theoretically, at least, all territorial authority in Bunyoro was held from the king and by his grace, and its grant implied enhancement of the recipient's ritual status as well as of his political status. Nyoro royal ritual is best understood as the symbolic expression of royal authority, and one of its effects is to sustain and validate this authority.

The King and His People

We now consider the king's relations, both in traditional times and at the present day, with the more important of the various categories of persons who make up Nyoro society. These are the members of the royal Bito line and their two heads, the Okwiri and the Kalyota, the king's mother, his regalia keepers, domestic officials, and advisers, his territorial chiefs of various grades and, finally, his people at large.

The word "Bito" denotes one of Bunyoro's hundred or more clans; it also denotes the present ruling dynasty. These are not quite the same thing. Though all Bito have the same avoidance object or "totem" (the bushbuck), only those who can establish a real genealogical link with the Mukama are accorded special prestige, and the closer the relationship the greater the prestige claimed and acknowledged. It is these close kinsmen of the king who are generally meant when the Bito are referred to; members of the Bito clan who can show no such explicit connection are not distinguished socially from members of commoner clans. Those who can demonstrate patrilineal descent from a Mukama of a few generations back (rarely more than four) regard themselves as a distinctive hereditary aristocracy, among whom the most distinguished are the "Bito of the drum," the actual sons of a Mukama. There are still a good many of these important Bito; former kings had many wives, and some were notably prolific: Kabarega had over a hundred children, some of whom are still living.

In the past, most important Bito received large estates from the Mukama, together with the political rights which such grants implied. They were thus important territorial chiefs. Nowadays, as we shall see in Chapter 4, European influence has broken down the traditional association between rights over land and political authority, and it has at the same time radically altered the basis on which land is held. A consequence of this is that Bito are no longer, as a class, the wealthy and powerful group which they formerly were. But they still claim special privileges and prestige; and they still preserve, under the nominal authority of their head, the Okwiri, the ability in certain contexts to act as a group.

The Okwiri, the Mukama's "official brother," is traditionally the eldest son of the late king, and he is formally appointed by the new Mukama after his accession. He is said to "rule" the Bito as the king rules the country as a whole. Structurally his office is interesting in that it provides a way of "detaching" the king from the exclusive Bito group to which he belongs by birth, so making possible his identification with the whole kingdom, non-Bito as well as Bito. For the King is not directly concerned with Bito interests, which often conflicted (and still do) with those of the people as a whole; these are the business of the Okwiri. This official nowadays represents the Bito on the central council of the native government, and resolutions (which are rarely if ever adopted) claiming for them special rights and privileges are still occasionally tabled through him. Even today, Bito claim special deference from commoners and are usually accorded it; many of them still hold large private estates which they administer autocratically; and they are sometimes said, not always without justification, to be arrogant and demanding, and heedless of others' rights. Like aristocracies elsewhere which have survived the political conditions in which they played an effective part, Bito still cling to the outward signs of an authority which they no longer have, and lord it over a peasant population which still shows little resentment. It might be thought that Bito, anxious for the reality of power, would have found places for themselves in the modern chiefly service. But very few have done so. This is consistent with traditional Bito values; service in the modern Nyoro government would involve official subordination to non-Bito, and to some of the more old-fashioned, this would be intolerable.

Corresponding to the Okwiri's position as the head of the Bito "princes" is that of the king's "official sister," the Kalyota. She is a chosen half-sister of the king (she has a different mother), whom he appoints to be the head of the Bito women or "princesses." These royal ladies enjoy a prestige similar to their brothers'. They were, indeed, said to be "like men," for like the princes they ruled as chiefs over the areas allotted to them. Formerly they were not allowed to marry or bear children; this helped to preserve the unity and exclusiveness of the king's lineage, for it prevented the growth of lines of sisters' sons to the royal house. To old-fashioned Nyoro, it would have been unthinkable for persons of such high status to assume the markedly subordinate status of wives. Today, however, the king's daughters, like other

Bito women, may marry and have children, but they usually marry men of high social standing who can afford to keep servants, for Bito princesses do not dig or carry water like ordinary women. Bridewealth is not paid in such marriages, for that would imply some degree of social equality. "How," an informant asked, "could a Bito and a commoner haggle about bridewealth? A Bito's word should be an order."

Like the Okwiri, then, the king's official sister was really a kind of chief; her appointment to office included the handing over to her of certain regalia, and like other persons succeeding to political authority she underwent the ceremony of "drinking milk" with the Mukama. She held and administered estates, from which she derived revenue and services, like other chiefs. She settled disputes, determined inheritance cases, and decided matters of precedence among the Bito women. She was not, as she is sometimes thought to have been, the queen, if by queen we mean the king's consort. It is said that in former times the Mukama could sleep with her if he wanted to, but he could do this with any of his royal sisters, so long as she was born of a different mother from his own. We may best regard her, then, as a kind of female counterpart of the king—the head of the Bito women, and so the chief lady in the land. We may see her office, like that of her brother the Okwiri, as one of the means whereby the royal authority was distributed. Though there is little place for her in the modern system, she still holds official rank, and her status is constitutionally recognized (as is the Okwiri's) by the payment to her of a small salary under the Bunyoro Agreement. Nowadays she is socially overshadowed by the king's true consort, the Omugo, whom he married in Christian marriage and who has borne him several children. It was she, not the Kalyota, who accompanied the Mukama on his visit to England for Queen Elizabeth's coronation in 1953, and she sits at his side at ceremonies and entertainments at which Europeans are present.

As in some other African monarchies, the king's mother also traditionally had considerable power, and kept her own court and ruled her own estates. She no longer has such authority today, but she is still much honored, and like the Okwiri and the Kalyota she receives a small official salary.

I referred above to the numerous regalia keepers and other palace officials who traditionally surrounded the king. Even today there are a great many such persons. Some are salaried officials; others, whose services are required only occasionally, receive gifts from the Mukama from time to time. These officials include the custodian of the royal graves, men responsible for the more important of the royal drums, caretakers, and "putters-on" of the royal crowns, custodians of spears, stools, and other regalia, cooks, bath attendants, herdsmen, potters, barkcloth makers, musicians, and many others. The more important of them have several assistants, and their duties are not onerous, for the care of a particular spear or attendance on the Mukama on ceremonial occasions occupies only a small part of a man's working life. This complex establishment is therefore not to be understood simply as an overcumbersome attempt to run a large household; neither in ancient times nor now can it be regarded as an economical or even as a particularly efficient way of doing this

Sociologically, the point of it is that it provided a means of involving a great many different groups and kinds of people in a common interest in the royal establishment and so in the maintenance of the kingship itself. It did this both through the clan system (for different offices were often hereditarily vested in particular clans, all of whose members shared in the honor of representation at the palace) and through occupational specialization (since it meant that all of Bunyoro's crafts were represented at the capital). In these ways the huge royal establishment served to integrate the Nyoro people around their center, and so to sustain the political system itself. Even in modern times prestige still attaches to these occupations, even where they are part time and unpaid, and I know of young men who have refused to take up profitable employment elsewhere in order to retain them. Moreover, a man who had served for some years in the palace might hope, if he gained the Mukama's personal favor, to be rewarded with a gift of an estate somewhere in the kingdom, thus becoming a kind of minor chief over its peasant inhabitants. Grants of this kind have been made even in recent times, though they have latterly rather taken the form of appointment to minor official chiefships. Such grants are not appropriate to a modern "civil service" type of administration; we shall return to this point.

In addition to this large body of palace and domestic officials, there was a loosely defined category of informal advisers and retainers. As well as certain officials in the last category, these included diviners and other persons who had attached themselves to the Mukama's household as dependants. These informal and private advisers had no official standing and they did not receive salaries. Some of them have, in the past, exerted considerable influence, and they have sometimes been said to be "nearer to the king" than the official chiefs. They acted at times as intermediaries between the chiefs and the king. They might expect to receive informal rewards from time to time, and they, too, might have received estates or minor chiefships for their services.

A much more important category of persons in traditional Bunyoro were the "crown wearers." To men whom the king wished specially to distinguish he gave elaborate beaded headdresses, with fringes or "beards" of colobus monkey skins. The award of a crown implied the grant of very high dignity and ritual status (recipients had to observe the same food restrictions as the king himself and were said to have a great deal of *mahano*). At the same time it involved accession to high political authority over considerable territories. Like other important chiefs the crown wearers had to take an oath of loyalty to the king, and to undergo the milk-drinking rite referred to above. In the past, crowns were awarded to persons who had performed some considerable service for the Mukama, such as winning a major victory in war; a crown was also traditionally awarded to the head of the king's mother's clan. Crowns, once awarded, were hereditary in the male line. The Bunyoro Agreement still provides for the grant of this award, which it describes as "an old-established order of distinction," but the institution is now falling into disuse, and no crown has been awarded for many years. The high ritual value that formerly attached to the Mukama's political authority no longer does so to the same extent, for such authority is seen nowadays to derive from other and more potent outside sources.

The system of territorial chiefship is discussed in the next chapter; here we need only note that traditionally all political authority was seen as deriving from the person of the king himself; as in feudal Europe, chiefs held their territories as gifts from the king, and this implied a close bond of personal dependence and attachment between him and them. Chiefship was essentially territorial; a chief was a person to whom the Mukama had granted rights over a particular territory and its inhabitants. These rights, even where they tended to become hereditary, were held only by the Mukama's favor: they could be withdrawn by him at any time, and sometimes they were. Though it does not seem that in pre-European times there was any such formal political hierarchy as there is now, there were different ranks of chiefs, from the great rulers of areas which roughly correspond with present-day counties, to minor chiefs with only a handful of peasant dependants.

This personal way of looking at the relationship between a ruler and his subordinates was quite appropriate to the relatively simple, "feudal" organization of pre-European times. Where political office is thought of as the sovereign's gift, it is important to seek and retain his personal favor, and it is natural that a return should be made for such a gift. If, even in modern times, chiefships should sometimes have been given, and promotion awarded, to persons who have rendered gifts or personal service to the king, and persons who have incurred his personal dislike should have been passed over, this would be wholly consistent with the values implicit in traditional Nyoro political structure, where personal attachment and loyalty were the supreme political values. It would be a serious mistake to regard such transactions, even now, as constituting breaches of tribal morality, although in terms of the impersonal standards of modern Western administration they are both wrong and politically harmful. It is natural, in such a system, that personal attachment should count for more than conformity to bureaucratic standards of efficiency and incorruptibility. And we must remember further that the exercise of political authority in pre-European times needed far less special training and knowledge than are demanded now. In Bunyoro, at all events, it is said that the expression of personal loyalty to the Mukama was until recent times hardly less necessary a qualification for political appointment than administrative experience or a high educational standard.

Appropriate though these attitudes were to the traditional system, they are plainly less so to modern times. Like other Western administrations, the British authorities are committed to encouraging the development of more modern and democratic political institutions, better adapted to the contemporary world of which Bunyoro is now a part. Traditional attitudes to chiefship are incompatible with these institutions. Many educated Nyoro realize this, and I have heard such people complain that faithful service in the Mukama's bathroom or kitchen is hardly an adequate qualification for even minor political office, and that the king's personal favor is not in itself an obvious qualification for the highest administrative posts. The situation, too, is greatly altered by the introduction of a cash economy, for when gifts formerly of kind are commuted to cash, they at once assume a different and more mercenary character. But it is an important part of the anthropologist's task to point out that such transactions are not properly understood when they are simply condemned as misdemeanors; rather, they have to be seen as usages surviving from a context in which they were proper and appropriate into one where they are no longer so. When values and patterns of behavior which are mutually incompatible come to coexist in the same rapidly changing political system, strains and conflict develop. We shall see in other contexts also that feudal values and bureaucratic ones do not always mesh smoothly.

Another example of uneasy coexistence of new and old values is found in the economic aspect of the relationship between the Mukama and his people at large. In the traditional system the king was seen both as the supreme receiver of goods and services, and as the supreme giver. Typically in systems of the Nyoro type, goods and services have to be rendered to the "lord," the person who stands next above one in the political hierarchy. Thus in Bunyoro the great chiefs, who themselves received tribute from their dependants, were required to hand over to the Mukama a part of the produce of their estates, in the form of crops, cattle, beer, or women. But everybody must give to the king, not only the chiefs. Even today the ordinary people make presents to him on certain ceremonial occasions. When he pays state visits to different parts of his country, as he often does, gifts of produce, for which there is a special Nyoro word, should be brought to him by peasants as well as chiefs. And larger gifts, in cash or kind, might be made to him from time to time by people who wish to obtain and retain his favor. All these various kinds of gifts express in traditional terms a kind of attachment between ruler and ruled which is important in a relatively small-scale feudal society. In addition, they formerly provided a sort of social insurance, for those who fell on hard times would naturally look for help to their chiefs and, ultimately, to the king.

The Mukama's role as giver was, accordingly, no less stressed. Many of his special names emphasize his magnanimity, and he was traditionally expected to give extensively in the form both of feasts and of gifts to individuals. But here, too, attitudes and values have survived the social conditions to which they were appropriate. People nowadays complain that the king no longer gives the great feasts which their grandfathers enjoyed. Their offerings of foodstuffs, they say, are taken away in a truck, and no feast, or at best a very inadequate one, is provided. They think that nowadays only the Mukama's circle of personal friends receives help from him. They do not see that the political changes of the past half-century, and in particular the advent of a cash economy, have made their attitudes and expectations anachronistic. For the truth is that the Mukama himself does not receive produce in the same quantities as his predecessors did, since the cultivators can now sell their surpluses for cash with which to satisfy their new needs. And to provide meat for huge feasts now, when cattle are virtually nonexistent and meat is prohibitively expensive, is economically impracticable. Also, as we have noted, many of the gifts which the Mukama now receives are in cash, not kind. And cash, unlike food and beer, does not have to be consumed quickly and communally in the form of gifts and feasts; it can be converted into many other desirable objects not formerly available. This state of affairs is not, of course, peculiar to Bunyoro; on the contrary, it is one of the most characteristic features of African kingdoms at the same stage of change. But in Bunyoro the economic aspect of political authority is particularly strongly institutionalized. It is thus inevitable that the incompatibility beween the traditional idea of rulers as centers for the collection and redistribution of goods, and the new pattern of bureaucratic authority which is now developing, should lead to bewilderment and strain. Nor should we be surprised that the nature of these conflicts is not always fully understood by those most closely involved in them.

4

The Chiefs

The Traditional System

IN THE TRADITIONAL Nyoro state all political authority stemmed from the king. Advised by his formal and informal counsellors, he appointed his territorial chiefs to office, and their authority, down to the lowest level, had to be confirmed by him personally. Traditionally, political office was not thought of as hereditary, though it often tended to become so. A chiefship could be taken away by the king at any time, but often it would be passed on to the original chief's heir. Chiefship, then, was not just a formal administrative office; rather, it was a private and personal (though conditional) possession, which like any other private property was thought of as hereditable.

The great chiefs had to maintain residences at the king's capital and to attend there constantly. This served as a check (though not always a very effective one) on rebellion. It also strengthened the group of advisers upon whom the king could rely; in political systems of this "feudal" type there was no need for a central secretariat, for the same people could serve both as royal councillors and as territorial administrators. When a chief was away from the court he had to leave behind him a representative or deputy, who assumed all his titles and took his place on ceremonial occasions. This use of deputies is characteristic of Bunyoro, as it is of the interlacustrine kingdoms generally; it may be said to express the dual quality of delegated political authority. For a territorial chief is essentially a "king's man," and so must be in constant attendance on him. But he is also a territorial ruler, personally responsible for the good administration of his area. To have a formal deputy to "double" for him provides a means of reconciling his two roles. Chiefs also had to provide the king from time to time with grain, beer, and cattle, as well as with ivory and other goods, and to supply men for work at the capital in peace time and for fighting in time of war. These exactions, of course, fell on the peasant population, and in return for them the peasants looked to their rulers for security and protection.

In the old days the chiefs did not occupy clearly distinguished grades, as modern chiefs do. They nevertheless fell into two broad categories. First there were the great chiefs who ruled over large areas and were answerable only to the Mukama; these probably included several crown wearers. Next there was a great number of lesser chiefs, having authority over very much smaller areas. These authorities could hold their areas directly from the king, just as the larger chiefs did, or they might be assistants or dependants of the major chiefs, to whom, rather than to the Mukama, they owed direct allegiance. But in either case their authority, like that of all persons wielding political power in the kingdom, would have to be formally validated by the Mukama. Below the dozen or so great *saza* or provincial chiefs, who ruled over definite regions of which the names and boundaries are still well known, chiefs seem not to have been thought of as occupying separate grades, but rather in terms of a gradual scale of power and importance. The status of any chief on this scale depended both on the number of subjects he governed and on the closeness of his relationship with the Mukama.

It does not seem that subordinate political authority in Bunyoro was ever a prerogative of members of the ruling Bito aristocracy. Some Bito did govern large chiefdoms, but most chiefs were either members of the respected Huma cattle-owning class, or people of commoner origin (though usually members of families with a tradition of chiefship). Usually a man was made a chief because he or one of his patrilineal forebears had earned the Mukama's gratitude either by service or by gift. The king often gave chiefships to his maternal or affinal relatives. In addition, palace officials and servants were often granted minor chiefdoms; as in the feudal states of medieval Europe, personal service to the king might bring a rich reward. Typically feudal, also, was the relationship of personal loyalty and dependence that existed between the king and his chiefs. In the language of modern sociology, the relationship between a political superior and his subordinate was "diffuse" rather than "specific"; that is, the chief's dealings with his subordinates were not restricted to a narrow official sphere, but extended over the whole of the subordinate's personal life. Even today many Nyoro feel that chiefs should be interested in them as persons, and not simply in their tax-paying or working capacity; we shall note later that the impersonal character of modern administration is a common ground for complaint.

One other aspect of the traditional Nyoro system must be discussed, and that is the connection between political authority and the possession of rights over land. The grant of a chiefship by the Mukama was essentially the bestowal of rights over a particular territory and the people in it. Nyoro did not think of these two things as being different; to be granted political authority was to be allotted an area in which to exercise it and of which to enjoy the profits, and to be given an "estate" was to be granted political authority over it. When, therefore, an ordered administration through chiefs was reintroduced early in the present century, it was natural that the persons appointed to chiefships should think of their areas as official "estates," from whose inhabitants they could exact goods and services for their support. With the introduction of money, the tribute paid by the peasant cultivators came to be commuted to an annual cash payment. This payment, which was seven shillings per adult male, was the chiefs' main source of revenue until the Bunyoro Agreement of 1933 provided that they should receive salaries instead. But in addition to the official chiefships, during the early 1900's the Mukama began to give plots of populated land to retired official chiefs as their private property, in reward for their services: chiefship was not then a pensionable office as it is now (at least in the higher grades). Similar gifts then began to be made increasingly to chiefs who were still in office, and also to members of the royal household, to palace officials, to Bito "princes" and "princesses," and to various other people whom the Mukama wished for one reason or another to favor. These gifts conformed with the traditional usage whereby the grant of minor chiefdoms provided a way for the Mukama to discharge his obligations toward persons to whom he was indebted. The estates or "fiefs" so granted were regarded as the private property of their owners, who enjoyed tribute and services from their occupants just as the chiefs did on their official estates. At about this time the quite new idea of unalienable, "freehold" tenure of land was gaining currency in Uganda, mainly owing to the terms of the Uganda Agreement of 1900, which—through a misunderstanding of the nature of the land rights involved—provided a large number of chiefs and other important people in Buganda with what amounted to freehold rights over considerable areas of land in that country. A consequence of this was that Nyoro fief holders came to think of their land rights not only as personal, but also as permanent and hereditable.

By 1931 a very large part of populated Bunyoro had been taken up in these private estates, the occupants of which found themselves subject not only to the official chief of the area, but also to the proprietor of the estate they lived in. Indeed these proprietors were regarded by their tenants no less as "chiefs" than the persons officially so designated. And the proprietors so regarded themselves, demanding from their peasant tenants the respect due their superior status. To a large extent they in fact fulfilled the role of chiefs; they settled disputes between their peasant tenants and often acted as intermediaries between their people and the official chiefs. The peasants themselves on the whole found nothing to resent in this arrangement. Indeed in some ways these landed proprietors have conformed more closely (they still do) to traditional Nyoro notions of what a chief should be than have the official chiefs themselves. For they are not, like the chiefs, liable to transfer, and their personal stake in the land gives them a closer interest in and knowledge of their "tenants" than is possible for a county or subcounty chief, much of whose time is taken up by court or office work, and whose stay in the area may be limited to a few years or less. Thus even today these proprietors may be said to fill a role not wholly filled by the lower grades of the official chiefs; they may even in fact find themselves in opposition to these officials, for village headmen sometimes resent the assured status and social prestige of the larger estate owners. Conversely, it is still popularly considered that the proper persons to

hold authority in these estates are their proprietors, and these proprietors sometimes resent interference in the internal affairs of their holdings by the government chiefs, whom they regard as "outsiders."

This widespread grant of private estates during the first quarter of the
century and afterwards was not, then, a proliferation only of estates and "land-
lords"; it was at the same time a proliferation of minor chiefs. In 1933 the
Protectorate Government tried, by legislation, to do away with these populated
estates, but the system of proprietary estates and the "feudal" way of thinking
which they implied were too deeply ingrained to be eradicated. Although the
official chiefs were now provided with salaries and were much reduced in
number, and although the exaction of tribute was now forbidden, large populated estates, even though no longer a source of profit, continued to be attrac-
tive. Their attraction was not, and never had been, mainly economic; it lay
rather in the enhancement of authority and status which their possession
implied. Hence the result of the 1933 reforms was not, as had been hoped, the
gradual disappearance of populated estates; it was, rather, the creation in the
popular mind of two kinds of chiefs, the salaried official ones and the proprietors of these estates.

From the point of view of the official chiefs, this dualism could only be
resolved by establishing themselves as authorities in both categories, and this
is exactly what they tried to do. Even today most official chiefs consider that
as well as administering their official chiefdoms they should also possess private
estates of their own. One of the first things a chief does on appointment is to
acquire a tenanted estate (if he does not already possess one) in some populated area not already claimed by somebody else. Almost all of the official
chiefs do possess such estates, mostly obtained, or their extent increased, after
their appointment or promotion. And the higher the chief's rank, the larger
the estate he is likely to possess; a county chief's estate may have up to fifty
occupying households, subchiefs average a little over a dozen, lower chiefs may
have five or six. The official chiefs are the largest single category of recipients
of populated estates, and they tend, also, to receive the largest areas.

Thus the traditional identity between political authority and the possession of personal and private rights over particular territories and the people
on them is still viable in Bunyoro. It has survived to a significant extent into
the increasingly "bureaucratic," impersonal kind of chiefship which is developing today. For Nyoro, a chief is still much more than an impersonal civil
servant, just as the proprietor of a populated estate is much more than a kind
of landlord. The nature of present-day chiefship, and the kinds of attitudes
toward it which exist, cannot be understood unless this is recognized.

I have applied the adjective "feudal" to Bunyoro's traditional political
organization. Let me conclude and summarize this section by comparing some
features of traditional Bunyoro with those characteristic of a typically "feudal"
state of medieval Europe. The term "feudalism" is usually applied to a medieval
European polity that is based on the relations of vassal and superior arising
from the holding of lands in feud—that is, in consideration of service and
homage from the vassal to his lord. England after the Norman conquest was

just such a state, and there is a striking resemblance between some of its political institutions and those of traditional Bunyoro.[1] We have seen that, in Bunyoro, lands were held and authority over them exercised very much on this feudal pattern. Even the beginnings of Norman feudalism in England are paralleled in Nyoro tradition. The Norman invasion of England was not a wholesale immigration; it was rather a conquest whose aristocratic leader won a kingdom for himself and distributed estates among his followers. Almost the same words could be used of the coming of the Bito to Bunyoro. Rukidi and his companions seem to have been a small group of Nilotic adventurers who took over the old Chwezi kingdom and divided it among themselves. There was no mass invasion of Nilotes; the Bito formed merely the "top layer" of a community which remained basically unchanged. In Bunyoro, too, the idea was fostered that all land belonged by right to the king, and could be held by others only as a gift from him, in reward for specified services. Personal loyalty to the king was all-important in both policies; in both, failure to render service when called upon was considered as rebellion and dealt with accordingly.

In twelfth-century England, feudal holdings were scattered about the country, so that a tendency on the part of any one of them to expand excessively would be checked by the others. In Bunyoro, the traditional allocation of territorial rights, and even the wide distribution of private estates during the first half of the present century, may be said to represent a similar policy. Further, the holders of European fiefs had to attend their lord's court when summoned; so also the great chiefs in Bunyoro had to be constantly present at the Mukama's headquarters, and even had to maintain permanent houses there. William I constantly traveled about the land with his entourage so as to secure the obedience of the more remote parts of the country. Likewise, in traditional times the court of the Mukama of Bunyoro moved often; it is only since the imposition of European rule in the present century that the king has had permanent headquarters. And he still makes lengthy tours of his kingdom, spending a week or more in certain places where an extensive though temporary replica of his palace is erected, complete with audience hall and living accommodation for himself and his entourage, at considerable local expense in time and labor. On these visits, too, he and his court are supposed to subsist on the gifts of food brought to him by his subjects.

We are told that William the Conqueror used to hold three great feasts yearly, at which he wore his crown and entertained in state. Great numbers of his lords and subjects would attend, thus both showing their loyalty and forming a body of advisers and assessors to the royal court. The Mukama of Bunyoro held one great feast yearly, attended by all the chiefs and many people, at which full regalia were worn and feasts provided.

---

[1] For the comparison which follows I have made particular use of D. Stenton's *English Society in the Early Middle Ages,* The Pelican History of England, Volume 3, 1955, which gives a short and readable account of English political institutions at and after the Norman conquest.

Like the English king, the Mukama of Bunyoro maintained a large body of palace and household officials, and these people were specially honored, as their counterparts were in medieval England. William often rewarded such dependants with an estate in land; we have seen that this, also, was the practice in Bunyoro. The English king, we are told, prohibited private war; the same thing was done in Bunyoro (as of course it must be where centralized political authority is enforced): it is said that in pre-European times blood vengeance could only be undertaken with the Mukama's consent, which might be withheld. We read that the English king tended to gather about him able men of commoner origin whom he sometimes ennobled for their services; similarly in Bunyoro any person could attach himself to the court and might achieve high office regardless of his hereditary standing. Finally, it was a tradition in Bunyoro, as it was in medieval Europe, for young men and boys to enter the households of people more eminent than themselves for their education. Even the Mukama's own sons were supposed to be brought up in the original home of some of the earlier Nyoro kings (now a part of the neighboring Toro kingdom), an area in which the aristocratic Huma clans were well represented.

Analogies are notoriously dangerous, the more so when they are drawn between peoples so remote from one another in space and time as the English of the Middle Ages and pre-twentieth-century Nyoro. But the resemblances between the two systems are sufficiently numerous and striking to make the feudal analogy an illuminating one, so long as it is critically used, and provided that the institutions which are compared are first of all analyzed and understood in their own proper contexts. After all, in a country with poor communications and a relatively low level of technological advancement there are certain natural limits to the possible ways in which a central authority can maintain any kind of orderly government. And perhaps the Bito rulers of Bunyoro faced problems of political organization and control not so very different from those which faced William and his Norman knights just nine hundred years ago.

The Modern Chief

Today, a Nyoro chief, whatever his rank, is a salaried official with specified duties. There are four grades of official chiefs; the county chiefs, the subcounty chiefs, the "parish" chiefs, and the village headmen. Each of the four county chiefs is responsible for an area of several hundreds of square miles, with an average population of around 25,000 people. Under each county chief there are four or more subcounty chiefs, each responsible for his division of the county. Every subcounty has two or three "parishes," each in the charge of a parish chief. At the lowest level are the village headmen, who are responsible for areas of perhaps two or three square miles, each containing a hundred or so people living in from forty to sixty or more households.

What men become official chiefs and how are they appointed? Though chiefship in Bunyoro is not hereditary, nonetheless a man who belongs to a family whose members have been chiefs has an advantage, for he knows something about the job and, also, he may be personally known to senior chiefs and perhaps even to the Mukama himself. Many chiefs are, in fact, sons or other relatives of former chiefs. Membership of the royal Bito clan is not by itself a qualification for appointment, and Bito are not particularly strongly represented in the ranks of the official chiefs. Traditionally, chiefs were simply men whom the Mukama had decided to make so. Essentially, they had to be people who had "made themselves known" to the Mukama, either through personal service or by being introduced to him by an existing chief or favorite. In recent times, although a candidate for chiefship must be acceptable to the Mukama, "achieved" as well as "ascribed" qualities are required. Thus for many years some degree of literacy has been an essential qualification, even for the lower grades. But there is a marked difference in educational level between the lower and the higher grades. In 1953 all except one of the county chiefs had been educated up to secondary standard, and so had just half of the subcounty chiefs; all had received primary education. On the other hand, less than a sixth of the parish chiefs had had secondary education, and no village headman had advanced beyond primary school. Nobody with secondary school education would take so humble a job as a village headmanship. In 1953 nearly half of the subcounty chiefs had been appointed from outside the service—that is, otherwise than by promotion from parish chiefships—and all except one of these had had secondary schooling. This new requirement of literacy in candidates for political appointment is obviously a major departure from traditional standards.

After the British conquest, chiefs were appointed by the European administration without much regard for the traditional system. But in 1933 the Bunyoro Agreement, which restored a limited degree of autonomy to the kingdom, gave the king authority to appoint and dismiss his own chiefs, subject only (in the case of the higher ranks) to the district commissioner's approval, and without consultation with his official Nyoro advisers. Though in fact the Mukama would usually take account of his chiefs' opinions and recommendations, an unintended effect of the Agreement was to personalize rather than to depersonalize the Mukama's relations with his territorial chiefs. Certainly when I was in Bunyoro, appointment and promotion in the chiefly service were said to depend hardly less upon the Mukama's personal favor than on such qualifications as experience and efficiency. It must be added here, however, that a new Agreement was concluded in 1955 (after my departure from Bunyoro), and this provides, *inter alia,* that chiefs shall be appointed and promoted only on the recommendation of special appointments committees, upon which non-officials as well as chiefs are represented. Thus the Mukama no longer possesses the powers in this respect which he previously had.

Before 1933 the main remuneration of chiefs came from money and goods paid to them as "tribute" by their peasant occupiers. In the case of the higher chiefs, this was supplemented by a rebate on the tax collected by them for the Government. The idea that chiefs should receive regular official salaries is thus a comparatively recent one. In 1953 the county chiefs had salaries of about £400 to £500 per annum, the subcounty chiefs from about £120 to £200, the parish chiefs from £30 to £40, and the village headmen less than £20 a year. For the lower grades of chiefs especially, these emoluments were quite inadequate to maintain the standards of living and hospitality appropriate to their positions. Salaries have been much increased since 1953, but village headmen and parish chiefs are still among the lowest paid employees in Bunyoro, and this is bound to affect adversely the esteem in which they are held by their people. County and subcounty chiefs may be given pensions on retirement; the two lower grades are not pensionable, though cash gratuities may be awarded after long service. The upper grades have free quarters provided for them by the Native Government, usually well-built permanent or semipermanent houses. Parish chiefs are also entitled to free houses, but these are usually ordinary mud-and-wattle houses like those of other villagers. Village headmen do not have free housing; they are usually local people, and it is assumed that they can continue to live in their own homes.

A chief's chances of promotion, especially from the lower ranks, are not great. A large proportion of the subcounty chiefs (about 40 percent of the total in 1953) are direct appointees who have never served as parish chiefs, and an even larger proportion of the parish chiefs have never been village headmen. The main reason for this incursion of "outsiders" at the middle levels is, of course, the need for the higher chiefs to be educated to a higher standard than formerly; almost all of the subcounty chiefs appointed from outside the service (and nearly half the total were so appointed) had had secondary education, unlike most of their colleagues who had risen from the ranks. An effect of this system is to keep most village headmen at the same level throughout their service, and also to diminish very much a parish chief's chance of becoming a subcounty chief.

Another important consequence of this dual mode of recruitment, especially at the subcounty level, is that some men who become chiefs in the higher ranks have little first-hand knowledge of or contact with the people. A county or subcounty chief lives in a small official world, with an office and courthouse, and a staff of clerks and messengers. These subordinates, together with the local parish chiefs and village headmen, inevitably tend to form a barrier between the higher chiefs and the peasant population, with whom they have relatively little direct contact at an everyday level. Unless such a chief has already had experience as a lower chief, he is bound to lack the intimate acquaintance with the details of day-to-day administration which his subordinates have. Of course subcounty chiefs do meet and tour among the people of their areas, but they do not live among them like parish chiefs and village headmen, who have neither offices, clerks, nor police, and who share the same kind of life as their peasant neighbors. Contact between county and subcounty chiefs and their people is also restricted by frequent transfer. Unlike men in the two lower grades, county and (especially) subcounty chiefs rarely remain in the same area for more than a year or two. It is hard for a chief to acquire an intimate knowledge of his district in so short a time, or to get to know more than a very few of its thousands of inhabitants. In contrast, parish chiefs often stay in the same parish for six years or more; ordinarily they are only moved on promotion to a subcounty chiefship, and such promotions are infrequent. Village headman are scarcely transferred at all except, rarely, on promotion; and they are almost always natives of the areas in which they are appointed.

What kind of work do chiefs do? There is a marked difference between the work of the two upper and the two lower grades. County and subcounty chiefs have to spend a lot of time on paper work; returns relating to tax collections, court cases, beer-brewing permits, food crops, vermin destruction, and many other matters have to be prepared and submitted monthly, and an extensive correspondence with superiors and subordinates has to be carried on. The formal hearing of criminal and civil cases in court may take one full day or more every week. All the chiefs are responsible for keeping order in their territories, for apprehending tax defaulters and other offenders, and for seeing that adequate food reserves are maintained. The collection of the annual tax is an urgent preoccupation, and it is common to see a subcounty or parish chief, with table, clerk, and policeman, established wherever money is being paid out—for example at cotton markets or tobacco-buying posts. All chiefs, but especially parish chiefs, spend a good deal of time in the informal settlement of village disputes "out of court."

The two lower grades of chiefs have much closer contact with the people than do the higher grades. Parish chiefs and village headmen have no office or clerical work to keep them at home, so they are constantly moving around among their people. They inspect growing crops, issue permits to brew the popular banana beer, supervise work on the roads and paths, organize and take part in communal hunts of such pests as wild pig and baboon, which do great damage to crops, tell cultivators where and what they should plant, summon people to court, and carry out innumerable other small day-to-day tasks. They are among and "of" the people in a way in which the higher chiefs cannot be, and it is through them that the force of Government is transmitted to the peasant population. One cannot fail to notice the informal way in which a village headman or even a parish chief drops in for a drink or a meal wherever he is visiting; when a subcounty chief is on tour, a very much more formal and constrained atmosphere prevails.

A formal system of advisory chiefs' councils was introduced some years ago. Under this system each chief, down to the parish level, has a panel of advisers who include, as well as the subordinate chiefs of the area, some popularly elected representatives of the people. These councils are supposed to meet at regular intervals, though they do not always do so. They all keep written records of their deliberations, and submit recommendations to the authority next above them. It was my impression in 1953 that the councils did not as yet have very much effect on the chiefs' decisions; this was no doubt partly because the principle of popular representation is likely to evoke only mild enthusiasm—to begin with, at any rate—where hierarchical and "feudal" values are as strongly entrenched as they are in Bunyoro.

The ways in which chiefs regard one another are in many respects more characteristic of the quasi-feudal traditional system than they are appropriate to a modern civil service. Internal differences in status are strongly emphasized. When a county or subcounty chief pays a formal visit to one of his subordinates, especially when he does so for the first time after appointment, the lower chief should give his superior a present of meat or cash, the amount depending on his rank. When a subcounty chief officially visits one of his parish chiefs or village headmen, there is usually a good deal of excitement. The premises are cleaned, everyone wears his best clothes, and food is specially prepared; the atmosphere is tense and formal. When a parish chief visits his village headmen, on the other hand, as of course he does constantly, there is no such formality. For these authorities live in the villages and are in daily contact with the people and with one another. Here again the cleavage between the remoter and more transient subcounty and county chiefs and the two lower grades is marked.

But all official chiefs, whatever their ranks, show a solid front to out-siders, who may include people of higher social and economic standing than (at least) the lower chiefs. Such are the proprietors of large populated estates, schoolteachers, clergy, members of the medical and other Government services, shopkeepers, and others. Political power, however, still rests mainly in the official hierarchy of chiefs, and this power has been used to suppress or at least to discourage adverse criticism or comment. Thus laymen are not encour-aged to bring complaints—of bribery or oppression, for example—against chiefs. In one court case a mission teacher accused a local village headman of accepting a bribe. The headman was acquitted, but the complainant was charged with slandering the village headman and was himself convicted. The judgment was not based on the truth or falsehood of the allegation of bribery; it was concerned with teaching the defendant that it was none of his business to criticize the village headman. Such criticism is only tolerable from an official superior. The insecurity of the lower chiefs' status vis à vis some of their wealthier and more distinguished subjects occasionally makes them sensitive about their official dignity and importance. It should not be inferred from this, however, that relations between the lower chiefs and the people are un-satisfactory; the case is very much otherwise. The point has been mentioned because friction does sometimes occur, and hence its underlying causes should be sought.

What do present-day Europeans and Nyoro expect of chiefs? As else-where in Africa, the European officials tend to look for efficiency in tax col-lection, expeditious handling of court work, quick despatch of correspond-ence and other business. Irregularities in the handling of cash are especially condemned, as are drunkenness and idleness. A bright and willing manner with Europeans is expected. The qualities that most Nyoro peasants look for are quite different. The traditional basis for their respect is the fact that the chiefs are the king's nominees, "the Mukama's spears." There must be chiefs, they say, for how otherwise could the country be ruled? Chiefs should be calm, dignified, and polite; they should not shout at their people or abuse them angrily. They should know their subjects and visit them often; people do not like a chief who sits in his office all day. Chiefs should be strong but not "fierce," and they should be generous and give frequent feasts and beer drinks.

Thus the qualities which European administrators and the mass of the Nyoro people look for in chiefs do not always coincide. A subchief whom I knew well was reported by touring European officers as being "a good chief with lots of drive and character," and "full of energy," but he was cordially disliked by his people for his jumpiness, lack of dignity, and abusive manners to his subordinates. The words "indolent" and "drinks too heavily" were applied to an older chief of good family and great Nyoro popularity who was less efficient by European standards. Since chiefs are expected to conform to two different and not always compatible standards, it is inevitable that they should be criticized by both Europeans and Nyoro. European criticism is mainly concerned with lapses from Western standards of good administration. Nyoro criticism is twofold, and itself reflects these dual standards. Older, less educated Nyoro criticize the chiefs for failing to conform to the traditional norms; younger men with European-inspired educations and ideals condemn them for failing to achieve what they think of as modern standards of democratic leadership. Thus older men often say that modern chiefs lack good family background, but are simply upstart commoners, who happen by some means or other to have won the Mukama's favor. Modern critics, too, have objected to the personal factor in the appointment of chiefs. Older men sometimes refer to the present-day chiefs as mere "hired laborers," implying that they are simply paid servants of the Government, concerned only with their salaries and prospects of promotion, and not interested, as chiefs traditionally were, in knowing and caring for their people as individuals.

It is commonly said that chiefs no longer provide feasts and beer parties for their people as they formerly did. The people who make this criticism do not always realize that a chief cannot do this unless his people bring him food and beer, for he certainly cannot do it on his salary. And such gifts are no longer brought as they used to be; when a man has paid his tax he considers that he has no further obligations toward his rulers, for tax is supposed to have replaced the old tribute payments, not to have been added to them. One old man shrewdly commented: "In the old days chiefs trusted and depended upon their subjects, for their living came directly from them. Now they do not care about their people, nor their people about them, for their money comes not from the people but from the Government." Nyoro are quite well aware of the degree to which the constant exchange of goods and services between people who know one another personally promotes social cohesion. Unlike such exchange, the annual payment of tax is a purely formal obligation; it involves no intensifying of personal relations. To the ordinary peasant it is simply a payment which he has to make to the Government and for which he receives no tangible return. Inevitably, then, chiefs are no longer bound to one another and to their people by the old ties of mutual and personal interdependence; they are more and more becoming impersonal civil servants—though, as we have seen, they are as yet by no means quite this. Everybody knows that times have changed, and the older and more traditionally minded regret it.

In summary, what is happening in Bunyoro is that the personal basis of political relations characteristic of the traditional system is being destroyed, and its place is being taken by the impersonal, bureaucratic organization which the efficient running of a complex modern society demands. But the changeover does not proceed evenly on all fronts, and we should not be surprised that attitudes and values appropriate to the older system still survive into, and may even modify, the new. Nor should we be surprised if the nature of these changes and the difficulties they give rise to are not always clearly understood by the people whom they most concern. Their most important practical consequence is that Nyoro chiefs, like chiefs in other emergent African societies, are expected to conform simultaneously to two separate and often incompatible sets of standards. Expectations regarding them are sometimes those appropriate to the "feudal" state which long ago ceased to exist in its traditional form; sometimes they express modern Western ideals by no means all of which have yet been fully assimilated. The Nyoro political system is no longer the traditional one, but neither is it the impersonal civil service which it is sometimes thought to be; it contains elements of both, together with features which are inconsistent with either. Chiefs are on the one hand respected because they are "the Mukama's spears"; on the other hand, they are despised because they are sometimes poorer and less educated than some who are not chiefs. They are praised by their European superiors and by the educated minority when they show efficiency and enterprise in carrying out their official duties; yet they are criticized by their subjects for failing to mix with them and to provide feasts for them as their predecessors did. They are expected, often, to be two different and incompatible things at the same time, and the remarkable fact is that they succeed so well.

$$\boxed{5}$$

Relatives

Kin

IN THE LAST TWO CHAPTERS we have been concerned with the Nyoro state,
the system of political relations which centers on the king and the hierarchy of territorial chiefs subordinate to him. This system, as we saw, not
only is an instrument of political control, but also, in its traditional "feudal"
form, implies a pervasive way of thinking about social relations. Central to
this way of thinking is the notion of superordination and subordination, the
idea that some kinds of people are naturally above or below other kinds of
people. But although these ways of thinking are characteristic of political or
"state" relations, they are not confined to the strictly political sphere. They
also pervade the community relationships which are to be our concern in this
and the following chapters. By community relationships we mean those day-
to-day relationships characteristic of village life, which subsist between near
neighbors and kinsfolk who not only live in the same place, but share common
interests and values and a common way of life.

In some of the simpler societies nearly everybody in a particular community is related by kinship to nearly everybody else. It is not quite like this
in Bunyoro. Though in any settled area a good many people do have relationships either of kinship or through marriage with a good many other people, a
man always has many neighbors who are neither kin nor related to him by
marriage. Thus Nyoro think of relationships of kinship and affinity,[1] and
relationships of neighborhood, as different, though of course they know quite
well that they may and often do coincide. We shall follow Nyoro themselves
in keeping the two topics separate. In the first part of the present chapter I
consider kinship, and in its second section I discuss marriage and the affinal

---

[1] *Affinal* relationships (substantive *affine;* abstract *affinity*) are what we call
relationships "in law"—that is, by marriage.

relationships to which it gives rise. I leave till Chapter 6 the consideration of those relationships which neighbors have and should have with one another even when they are not kinsfolk or affines.

Kinship is usually of great significance in the simpler societies which most anthropologists study, and hence social anthropologists attach much importance to it. Where a person lives; his group and community membership; who his friends are and who his enemies; whom he may and may not marry; from whom he may inherit and to whom pass on his property and status—all these considerations may depend upon kinship ties and be thought of in terms of them. Kin relationships are less important for Nyoro than they are for some peoples (though it is likely that they were more important in the past), but they are still significant in very many social situations.

The kinship basis of group membership is particularly important. A Nyoro inherits his clan name and associated totemic avoidance, his membership of a particular group of kinsmen, and, usually, his status and property, from his father. Nyoro say that in former times patrilineal descent determined membership of the actual groups of men who lived in particular territories, so that almost all the men in any particular settlement (which might be from one to three or more square miles in extent) would be related by descent in the male line from a common ancestor. Nyoro clans are exogamous, meaning that men must marry outside their clans, and wives come to live at their husbands' homes. Thus the married women in such localized descent groups or lineages would be of different clans from those to which their husbands belonged. Where residential and cooperating groups are formed in this way, loyalty to the other members of one's group is a most important social value.

However things may have been in the remote past, in Bunyoro nowadays the principle of unilineal descent[2] is no longer the most important factor which determines membership of territorial groups. But membership of a group of patrilaterally related kinsmen, or agnates,[3] is still very important in connection with personal loyalties, marriage and inheritance, and in various other contexts. Nyoro still attach high value to mutual devotion and support between agnates. Thus it is still thought proper for sons of the same father to build their houses near to one another and to maintain close and friendly relations, and many still do so. It is only by understanding the profound importance of this kind of *group* membership, and the wide range of social relations in which membership of such a group is important, that we can make sense of Nyoro ways of thinking about kinsfolk and affines, and in particular of their kinship terminology.

Nyoro kinship terminology is classificatory, like that of many simpler peoples for whom affiliation with a particular group of kin is important. This means, usually, that terms which one applies to relatives in one's own line of descent are also applied to certain other relatives who are in collateral lines

---

[2] *Unilineal* descent is descent reckoned through one line only—that is, either exclusively through males or exclusively through females.

[3] *Patrilateral* kinsfolk, also called *agnates* (adjective *agnatic*), are persons to whom one is related through males only.

of descent. Thus one's father's brother may be called "father," his son may be called "brother," and so on. Even a father's sister (who is a member of one's father's group and generation) may be called "father," and the Nyoro term for this relative can be translated "female father." As far as one's patrilateral relatives are concerned, this classificatory usage means that all of them, however distant the connection, are "brothers," "sisters," "fathers" (both male and female), "grandfathers," "children," or "grandchildren." And to call them by these terms means that one should behave toward them, to some extent at least, as one would toward one's nearest agnatic kinsfolk in these various categories. In Bunyoro this usage even extends to people with whom no genealogical relationship at all can be traced, for any member of one's own clan (and clans are widely dispersed and often no real genealogical relationship can be traced between clansmen) is regarded as an agnatic relative, and placed in the appropriate generation. One of the effects of this classificatory usage is to enhance and stress the unity of groups of agnates, for it implies that the same kind of cooperation and mutual support should be extended to and expected from all its members, whatever the degree of relationship. Indeed it would be unseemly to inquire about the exact relationship; Nyoro say that where clansmen are concerned the important thing is friendship, not the degree of relationship.

But the classificatory system is not restricted to one's agnates. A man's mother's sister (who of course is not his agnate, since her link with him is not through his father but through his mother) is regarded as a kind of mother, and is so referred to. His mother's sister's children, like his own mother's children, are called "brother" and "sister." Even his mother's brother is a kind of "mother" (even though he is a man), and he is called "male mother." This is not so strange as it sounds, when it is remembered that the most important thing about your mother's brother is that he is a member of the same agnatic group or lineage to which your mother belongs. In quite a real sense *all* the members of your mother's agnatic group are "mothers": your attitude toward them is quite different from your attitude toward your "own" people, the group of agnates of which you yourself are a member. In systems like the Nyoro one, where one's father's people (and so one's own) and one's mother's people belong to quite separate and distinct social groups and are quite differently regarded, it would evidently be most misleading to translate the words for both father's and mother's siblings (that is, brothers and sisters) as "uncles" and "aunts," as we do in our system. We use, for instance, the same term, "uncle," for both father's brother and mother's brother, because we think of them both as the same kind of relative. To Nyoro, on the other hand, they are as different as can be, for one's father's brother is a member of one's own group, while a mother's brother is a member of an entirely different group. And a Nyoro's expectations and obligations in regard to members of these two distinct groups are quite different.

These ways of classifying kin provide a means of placing in a few simple categories a great many of the people whom a Nyoro peasant is likely to have dealings with in his everyday life. Everybody he meets is either a member of his own clan or he is not. If he is, he must be treated as a father, a brother, or a son, depending on their relative ages. If he is not, he may be a member of a clan with which the speaker is related through either kinship or marriage. Thus he may be a member of his mother's clan and so a kind of mother, or of a grandmother's clan and so a kind of grandmother, or of his wife's or his brother's wife's clan and so a kind of brother-in-law. Or he may belong to a clan in which there is another member with whom the speaker or one of his clansmen has made a blood pact, in which case friendliness and mutual help are prescribed. In all these cases there is a ready-made set of behavioral categories, labeled with kinship or affinal or "blood-partnership" terms, through which amiable personal relations may, and should, be established and maintained. In these ways the Nyoro clan system, combined with the classificatory mode of designating relatives, provides for the extension of a few quite simple relationship categories over a very wide social field.

In considering kinship, it is particularly important to bear in mind that one is dealing not simply with a set of abstract concepts, but with real people and the ways in which they act toward and think about one another. Hence before discussing the different kinds of social behavior which are prescribed between different kinds of kin, I must say a few words about Nyoro territorial and domestic organization. A Nyoro homestead usually consists nowadays of a rectangular four-room house, with mud-and-wattle walls and a thatched roof. Some wealthier people have brick houses roofed with iron. In remoter areas the old-fashioned "beehive" type of house is still common. The homestead faces on a central courtyard of beaten earth, around which there are usually one or two subsidiary buildings: a kitchen, a smaller house or two for second or other wives if the household is polygynous, and nowadays a small latrine. The home is usually surrounded by food gardens interspersed with fallow land, and often a shady banana grove adjoins the house. There are probably other similar households not very many yards away. A number of such scattered homesteads make up a settlement area or "village." Such villages may occupy a square mile or more, and they are often separated from other similar, settled areas by narrow winding streams or by swamps or by unoccupied bush. Three or four such settlements may make up the area administered by the lowest grade of territorial chief, the village headman.

The average homestead nowadays contains four or five people, though some households are considerably larger. The basic domestic unit is generally the elementary family of a man, his wife, and their children, though this pattern is modified when a man has more than one wife and so is the head of two elementary families, or when an adult son continues to live in his father's household after he is married; though this last is still the ideal Nyoro pattern it is not now very common. Other relatives, such as an unmarried brother or sister of the household head, or one of his wife's kinsfolk, may also stay in the homestead for longer or shorter periods.

The family head, or (as Nyoro call him) the "master of the household," is much respected. This is what we should expect in socially stratified Bunyoro. People say that he "rules" the household just as the Mukama rules the whole country. He is the master and ultimate owner of everything the household contains; even property which is apparently at the disposal of his adult sons is, strictly speaking, his. Though nowadays the traditional authoritarian pattern is tending to break down, and sons, like wives, are becoming increasingly independent owing to the opportunities which they now have to grow cash crops and take paid employment, the very high status of the household head is still an important Nyoro value. This is made especially clear when we consider the relationship between fathers and sons.

Though there may be genuine affection between them, Nyoro culture stresses the authority of the father and the dependence and subordination of the son. A son should always be polite and deferential, and he should address his father as "sir" or "my master"—the very same terms that he would use to a chief. A man should not sit on a chair or stool in his father's presence; he should sit or squat on the floor. He should not marry a girl whom his father has not selected for him, or at least approved. He should never wear any of his father's clothes or use his spear. And he may not begin to shave or smoke until he has made a small token payment to his father. Thus the relationship is essentially an unequal one, and it may even be said to express a latent hostility between fathers and sons. Such hostility is to be expected in a strongly patrilineal society, where the father's very considerable authority and status pass on his death to his son. It is as though the son's growing up were a kind of challenge to the father, whose authority the son will soon take over; and the father seems accordingly almost to resent his son's developing adulthood as a threat to his own preeminence.

The pattern of Nyoro inheritance is consistent with the existence of such attitudes as these. The heir (who should not be the oldest son) is ceremonially installed in the presence of his agnates. The ceremony stresses the transfer of authority rather than the transfer of property, and the heir is even said to "become" his father. Indeed after he has been installed his sisters' husbands should address him as "father-in-law," not as "brother-in-law" as they formerly did, and they should treat him with great respect. It is also of significance that in Bunyoro there can be only one heir; the household and the patrimonial land are never divided up (though movables may be), for they are indivisible, like the parental authority which they symbolize.

The relations between fathers and daughters express the same theme of superordination and subordination; a father "rules" his daughters just as he rules everyone else in his household. Indeed a daughter is doubly subordinate, for as well as being a child she is also a woman, and women should always be subservient and respectful to men. She will marry elsewhere, and the bridewealth which is obtained for her may be used to obtain a wife for her brother, perhaps even another wife for her father himself. Her children will not increase her father's posterity; they will belong to another clan, her husband's. In traditional times, at least, her feelings were not much considered in marriage. Even today fathers sometimes try to compel their daughters to stay with uncongenial husbands, so that they will not be called upon to return the bridewealth which they have received for her. The relationship between fathers and their children, then, is one of marked inequality: fathers "rule" their children and children "fear" their fathers. It follows from what was said earlier that the relationship with father's brothers, or "little" fathers, is similar; even father's sisters, or "female fathers," are thought of as being rather severe, like fathers, and quite different from one's mother and her sisters, with whom the relationship is much more friendly and intimate.

We have noted that the term which we translate "mother" is applied to one's mother's sisters as well as to one's mother, and even (with a masculine suffix) to one's mother's brother. It is even applied to one's mother's brother's children, whom we should call our matrilateral cross-cousins,[4] and to one's mother's brother's sons' children. The explanation of this peculiar usage is that all these relatives are members of the same agnatic descent group as one's mother, and so are all thought of as "mothers." The child of one's mother's sister is not a "mother," for she belongs to a different lineage and clan from one's mother, since clans are exogamous. The child of a mother's brother's daughter is not a "mother" for the same reason. A Nyoro thinks of himself as the child of the *whole agnatic group* of which his mother is a member, and he therefore thinks of all its members, even men and persons younger than himself, as being in a sense his "mothers." From all the relatives whom he calls "mother," and especially from the women, he looks for love and indulgence. Nyoro often contrast the friendly intimacy of the mother-child link with the comparatively strict and authoritarian relationship between children and their "fathers." Men have a very keen affection for their mothers, and aged women often live with their adult sons. This friendly intimacy also characterizes the relationship between men and their real or classificatory "male mothers"; a sister's child may make much freer with his mother's brother's property than he can with his father's; for example, he may help himself to food or borrow clothes or other property without formality in his "male mother's" house. Nyoro often say how happy they were when they visited their mothers' people as children. There is, nonetheless, an undercurrent of hostility in the relations between men and their mothers' brothers; we shall see why this should be so when we discuss affinal relationships in the next section.

A Nyoro thinks of his father's brother's children, and of his mother's sister's children, as relatives of the same kind as his own father's and mother's children respectively—that is, as his own brothers and sisters—and he so refers to them. When he wishes to distinguish between his real or classificatory siblings on his father's side and those on his mother's side, he does so by calling them "children of my father" and "children of my mother" respectively. Between sons of the same "father" the stress is, as we might expect, on mutual solidarity and support. Brothers should help one another in quarrels, they should build near to one another, and they should help to take care of one another's children. There are terms for distinguishing older and younger siblings, but a

---

[4] *Matrilateral* kinsfolk are persons to whom one is related through females only. *Cross-cousins* are the children of a brother and a sister. (Children of two brothers or two sisters are called *parallel cousins*.)

brother is not especially respected because he is older. When, however, one brother becomes his father's heir (which he may do while still quite young), the other brothers must treat him with the deference due a household head. But despite the stress on solidarity, Nyoro are realists, and they recognize that brothers sometimes hate and are jealous of one another. There is a Nyoro saying to the effect that when a man becomes rich he treats his brother as an inferior, and it is true that a wealthy man may resent the claims made upon him by less fortunate fellow clansmen. Nyoro are well aware that social relationships may be ambivalent; they realize that inconsistent attitudes and patterns of behavior very often coexist in the same relationship.

It is natural that Nyoro should attach great importance to good brotherly relations, for the idea that agnates should stick together and support one another is central to the traditional pattern of local territorial grouping. Sisters, of course, do not form groups in this way, for when they grow up they marry into other families and separate. It is significant that although Nyoro often use the word for "brotherhood," one never hears a corresponding word for "sisterhood." In the context of group relations there is no occasion for such a concept, for although sisters often maintain friendly relations throughout their lives, the nature of the Nyoro social system makes it impossible for them to form corporate groups as their brothers do.

Brothers and sisters usually maintain close and friendly relations throughout life. They grow up in close contact, and there is not the competition for authority that there is among brothers. They may talk freely to one another about their affairs, including sexual ones. A boy may jokingly address his sister as "wife," for he perhaps will marry with the bridewealth which is received for her. But he must not sleep with her; that would be incest and would bring about a condition of grave ritual danger.

We noted above that Nyoro think of their fathers' brother's children and their mothers' sister's children (relatives whom we think of as cousins) as brothers and sisters. But they think quite differently about the children of their fathers' sisters and the children of their mothers' brothers (relatives whom we think of as cousins too), and they have quite different terms for them. They are not thought of as siblings at all. One calls one's mother's brother's son and daughter "male mother" and "little mother" respectively, just as one calls one's mother's brother and sister, and one calls one's father's sister's children "children"—though one distinguishes them terminologically from "children" in one's own clan. This odd usage, which seems to put one's matrilateral cross-cousins in the generation above and one's patrilateral cross-cousins in the generation below one's own respectively, is sometimes called the Omaha system of cross-cousin terminology, after an American Indian tribe among whom it was long ago recorded. Though puzzling at first sight, it is really quite simple when it is realized how important membership of a particular descent group is for many peoples throughout the world. When grouping is based on agnatic descent, one's mother, her brother, and her brother's children are all in the same descent group, and this is one of the most important things about them. Thus, as we noted above, a man thinks of himself as a child not only of his mother, but also, in a sense, of his mother's group as a whole. All the members of that group are therefore "mothers," either male or female. If you look at the relationship from the other end—that is, from the point of view of a member of the agnatic group of "mothers"—your father's sister's children, no less than your sister's children, are your "children." What is happening here is that you are identifying yourself with your own agnatic lineage as a whole, so the child of any woman of that lineage (whether of your sister or your father's sister or even of your father's father's sister) is also your own "child," and you are its "mother." Of course such "children" are not the same as one's own children, for they belong to another clan. Hence Nyoro have a separate term to distinguish them.

A word should be said about the relationship between grandparents and grandchildren. In accordance with the classificatory usage which I have described, a grandfather's siblings are called "grandfather," regardless of sex, and a grandmother's siblings are called "grandmother," regardless of sex. Indeed all the members of both parents' mothers' lineages (who are all "mothers" —either male or female—to each of the parents) are called "grandmothers." Thus the odd fact that Nyoro may have male "grandmothers" and female "grandfathers" makes sense when the essentially "group" reference of Nyoro kinship terms is understood. Further, the assertion that Nyoro can marry their grandmothers seems less bizarre when we realize that what is meant is that it is permissible for a man to marry into his father's mother's clan.

The relations between grandparents and grandchildren are friendly and intimate, contrasting strongly with those between fathers and sons. A boy may joke and play with his grandfather in a way which would not be permissible with his father, and Nyoro grandparents, like their Western counterparts, are often said to "spoil" their grandchildren. We spoke earlier of the incipient hostility between fathers and sons; grandfathers have already been replaced by their sons, and so are, as it were, out of the battle. Nyoro sometimes say that grandfathers are "like brothers," thus stressing the equality and friendliness of the relationship.

Marriage and Affinity

Nyoro think of marriage as a more or less permanent union between a man and a woman, the offspring of whom have recognized status as their children. Ideally marriage should involve the payment of brideweath (formerly in cattle, now in cash) and the establishment of enduring relations between the husband and his wife's people. Even where no bridewealth is paid, the children still belong to the father's clan and lineage, but the husband's status, especially in regard to his in-laws, is then much lower. Bridewealth nowadays averages about ten pounds, which is quite a lot of money in a community where most peasants' cash incomes during a year hardly exceed this amount. Most marriages are monogamous, but Nyoro still like to have two or more wives if they can afford it, and even Christians sometimes have another wife besides their "church" or "ring" wife. A Nyoro may not marry into his own, his mother's, or his mother's mother's clan; he may marry into his father's mother's clan, provided that the relationship is not too close. Nyoro approve of marriage with neighbors; they say that it is a good thing to know something about one's prospective wife and her family before one becomes engaged. Most marriages are still between families who live within a day's walk of each other; this means that most people have affines within easy reach and see them often.

In pre-European times most marriages were arranged by the parents. Nowadays many still are, although young people often choose their own mates. Marriages could be arranged while the intended partners were still children, or even before they were born. In this latter case, a man might say to a close friend: "My wife is pregnant; I give her child to you!" He would mean by this that if his child were a girl his friend could have her as a wife for his son, provided of course that he paid bridewealth for her. If the child turned out to be a boy there would be no marriage, though the boy might become a kind of dependant in his father's friend's household. For a man may give away women and slaves, but he cannot give away husbands. This traditional antenatal betrothal illustrates two important points. First, it shows that traditionally the woman is not one of the two contracting parties in marriage; she is rather the subject of a transaction between two men and the groups of kin they belong to. Secondly, it stresses the fact that for Nyoro the woman's group is always the giver and the husband the receiver. And the giver always has superior status, while the receiver is subordinate and must be humble and respectful to his prospective in-laws. This is still so today, even when bridewealth has been paid. Nyoro theory is that however large the bridewealth, it can never balance the inestimable gift of a woman, who will bring to her husband's group both her labor and, most important of all, her capacity to bear him children to continue his line.

In traditional Nyoro marriage (to which even today most marriages conform) a number of formalities have to be carried out which extend over many weeks and even months. First, the prospective bridegroom, accompanied by a few kinsmen, pays a formal visit to the bride's father's home, bringing a gift of a large goat and some jars of banana beer. Everyone is dressed in his good clothes and is on his best behavior. The bridewealth to be paid is discussed. The suitor and the girl's father do not engage in direct negotiations; all discussion is carried out through intermediaries, for it would be unseemly for the prospective father-in-law to stoop to what might become acrimonious wrangling about the amount of bridewealth to be paid. Often a pretext is found for "fining" the bridegroom or a member of his party for some real or imagined impropriety in the past; the aim is to show that they are uncouth, worthless people, unfit to receive a woman from the host group. Other pretexts may be found for mulcting the bridegroom's party of a few more shillings. Throughout, the bride's group assumes an air of haughty superiority, and the bridegroom's party accepts a humble and deferential role.

Some weeks or months later a representative of the bride's family formally visits the bridegroom's father's home to collect the bridewealth. He is courteously received and given beer to drink. After collecting the money (for which he nowadays writes a receipt) he demands other small traditional payments, including some cents to repay him for the energy he expends in beating the bridewealth cattle along the road home (there are really no cattle, but there might have been long ago!). After another interval the main "giving away" ceremony is held. The bride is brought to her new husband's home after dark, accompanied by a group of her own and of her future husband's kinsfolk. Her head is veiled in barkcloth, and the procession moves slowly, taking an hour or more for the short journey. There is singing on the way, and many of the songs extol the great value of the gift that is being brought. When the husband's homestead is reached, the bride and bridegroom are ceremonially seated on the bridegroom's parents' laps, there is a ritual washing of the bride and groom, and the family's Chwezi spirits are invoked. That night the marriage may be consummated, and there is a feast which should continue for several days and nights.

On the next morning the relatives of both parties assemble, and a letter from the bride's father (who is not himself present) is read out by his representative. The letter is in conventional form and instructs the bridegroom's father (not the bridegroom himself) to treat the girl well, not to punish her with undue severity, to permit her to visit her relatives, and so on. It is read out in a threatening and passionate manner, and the bridegroom's father replies humbly. Others of the bride's family may add their own admonitions to what has been said. Some days later the bride returns to her father's house, where she spends several days before going back to her husband with gifts of food from her family.

To an observer of the complex series of rites involved in traditional Nyoro marriage, what is most striking is the strong emphasis on the different statuses of the two groups involved. This status difference is strongly marked in the relations between the husband (and his close agnates) and all his wife's agnates, but before we consider these relationships a word must be said of the husband-wife relationship. We have already noted the high status of the household head; this is particularly marked in his relations with his wife or wives, for men are always superior to women. Most of the domestic and farm work falls to women; a wife is required always to be submissive and deferential to her husband; she should kneel to hand him anything, and should address him as "sir." But she is by no means a slave; she has definite rights, and between many spouses there are very close bonds of affection. Her husband must provide her with a house, clothes, and a hoe to dig with; if he fails in his obligations, or constantly neglects or abuses her, she may complain to her own people and in the last resort she may leave him, provided that her people are able and willing to return the bridewealth paid for her. Nyoro men are nowadays much concerned about the increased economic independence which a woman can gain through growing and selling cash crops, because it means that she can, if she wishes, repay her own bridewealth and leave her husband on what he may consider an inadequate pretext, or indeed on no pretext at all.

A man feels constraint in the presence of his wife's people; he must always be polite and formal in his dealings with them (as they should be with him), and he should, in particular, avoid seeing or talking to his wife's mother. He and his brothers refer to his wife's people as "those who make us feel ashamed"; they mean that they would feel ashamed if they behaved overfamiliarly or discourteously to them. Nyoro themselves explain this restraint by pointing out that a man and his wife's agnates belong to different descent groups. In his own group a man feels an easy assurance and a sense of security, but his wife's group are "strangers," and if they are offended they may break off relations with him, which is something that his own agnates cannot so easily do, however greatly he offends them. Hence his attitude to his in-laws is ambivalent: on the one hand he feels gratitude and respect toward them, for they have given him a wife; on the other hand he is conscious of fear and even hostility toward them, for they are not his own people, but outsiders. He stands to his father-in-law, and so to his father-in-law's whole lineage, as a "child"; "the one who has taken our daughter." Hence from their point of view, also, the relationship is ambivalent: on the one hand a son-in-law is a "child," and children are to be not only loved but ruled, and they owe respect and obedience to their parents; on the other hand he is an outsider, who must be treated formally and politely.

A man has many obligations to his wife's father. He should visit him often, and bring him presents. He should help him in bush clearing, building, and other work, and he must always behave respectfully to him. If he fails in any of his obligations, his father-in-law may "fine" him (I have known of such cases). Nyoro often say, in the pervasive idiom of subordination and superordination, that men "rule" their daughters' husbands, and husbands often complain of the heavy demands their wives' fathers make upon them.

A man feels something of the same constraint even with his wife's brothers, one of whom is his father-in-law's heir and so will become his father-in-law when the father dies. But here the constraint seems to be mitigated by the fact that brothers-in-law are likely to be generational equals, and there is a friendly, give-and-take quality about the relationship which is not found in affinal relations between members of successive generations. But a formal element still exists there, at least when the different group membership of the parties to the relationship is relevant, as it is, for example, when formal visits are exchanged. And brothers-in-law should always be polite to one another, and give one another gifts. In a man's relations with his wife's sister, however, this formality is conspicuously lacking, for he feels toward her something of the intimacy and familiarity that characterize his relationship with his own wife. She may even jokingly be called "wife," and a man can marry two sisters if he likes; I know of several polygynous unions of this kind. The fundamental inequality which exists between the wife-giving and the wife-taking groups thus is modified in the relationship between a man and his wife's siblings, especially his wife's sisters. Here the status difference between the two parties seems to be submerged beneath the closer affective ties which the husband-wife bond implies.

It remains to consider the relationship between men and their sisters' children. I said above that this topic would be more suitably considered in an affinal context, and perhaps it is already plain why this should be so. Nyoro themselves often compare the mother's brother—sister's son relationship with the affinal one. They point out that a sister's son, like a daughter's husband, is "a man from outside," for of course he derives his clan and lineage membership from his father, who is "son-in-law" to his mother's lineage. We noted that there was constraint in the relationship between men and their daughters' husbands, and Nyoro see something of the same constraint as being carried on (on both sides) into the following generation—that is, into the relationship between men and their sisters' children. But as well as being an outsider, a sister's child is also a "child" to his mother's group in quite a literal sense; unlike a son-in-law he is a blood relation and, as we saw, all the members of his mother's lineage are "mothers" to him. So the relationship is ambiguous; in English we should have to say that the sister's son is thought cf both as a kinsman and as an affine at the same time. The relationship thus implies both familiarity and constraint, and these two attitudes are not entirely compatible with one another. Let us see how Nyoro culture deals with this potentially difficult relationship.

First of all, friendly intimacy between men and their mothers' brothers is much stressed. A man may make himself quite at home in his mother's brother's house. He may borrow almost anything he wants without asking, and he may help himself to food uninvited. His mother's brother's wife must always prepare a meal for him if he asks for one; if she fails to do so he may stamp on the three hearthstones where she cooks, and if he does this, it is believed that food will never cook properly on that hearth again. The sister's son has a right to the head of any animal killed by his mother's brother, and he can also claim a payment when any girl of his mother's brother's lineage marries, for he is being deprived of a "mother." We noted above that Nyoro often speak of the happy time they spent at their mothers' brother's homes when they were children. But as well as this friendly intimacy there is an undercurrent of antagonism, and this is expressed in certain ritual prohibitions to which the sister's son is subject. Thus he must not sit on or kick the cooking stones in his mother's brother's house, on pain of the consequences we have just noted. He may not sit on the grinding stone; if he does, his uncle's teeth may fall out. He may not climb on to his mother's brother's roof, nor walk through his growing crops, nor should he take hold of anything new in his mother's brother's house. And he may not climb on to his mother's brother's bed, or sleep with his wife. It is interesting to note that if the sister's son commits any breach of these prohibitions it is not he but his uncle who will suffer for it: in the idiom of superordination and subordination, Nyoro say that a man "rules" his mother's brother. It is significant that a sister's son's ghost is much feared, and so is his curse. It appears that political and social inferiority may sometimes be compensated for by the attribution of ritual power to the occupant of the inferior status; if this is so, then in Bunyoro the ritual power which a man has over his mother's brother may be regarded as a compensation for the inferiority of status thrust upon his father by his wife's people.

Thus a man loves, yet fears, his sister's son. The latter "rules," but acknowledges ritual restrictions in regard to his mother's brother. One's sister's son, like one's daughter's husband, is an outsider, since he belongs to a different clan and lineage from one's own. But at the same time, unlike a daughter's husband, he is your "child," for you are a member of his mother's agnatic group, and so his "mother." Children are loved, outsiders are feared; therefore one who is both is both loved and feared. That is why the mother's brother –sister's son relationship in Bunyoro is an ambivalent one. The symbolic restrictions which surround it provide a way of expressing and controlling this ambivalence.

Neighbors

Good Neighborliness

I TURN NOW to consider the ways in which Nyoro should, and do, behave toward one another simply as neighbors, whether or not they are kin to one another as well. Nyoro attach a high value to neighborliness. They like their neighbors to take an interest in them, and they tell the following story to illustrate this.

Once a man moved into a new village. He wanted to find out what his neighbors were like, so in the middle of the night he pretended to beat his wife very severely, to see if the neighbors would come and remonstrate with him. But he did not really beat her; instead he beat a goat-skin, while his wife screamed and cried out that he was killing her. Nobody came, and the very next day that man and his wife packed up and left that village and went to find some other place to live.

Nyoro like to live near one another, and on the whole neighbors get on well. But inevitably they sometimes do not. In the first part of this chapter I consider the kinds of rights and obligations which are involved in "neighborliness," and the ways in which village solidarity is expressed. In the second part I discuss some of the types of interpersonal conflict which arise in the Nyoro village community, and the kind of action which may be taken to resolve these conflicts.

Neighbors should help and support one another in their everyday occupations. A man who cuts himself off from his fellows and lives far away from other people in the bush is distrusted and may be suspected of being a sorcerer. When a man builds a house he expects help from his neighbors, and he should recompense them with a meal at the end of the day. Neighbors should help one another in agricultural work, especially in bush clearing and harvesting. Nowadays a group of neighbors (who may not be kin to one another at all) often combine for tobacco growing. They jointly cultivate and care for a common seedling nursery, and sometimes they plant out the seedlings in a large communal field which they have together cleared of virgin bush. The obligation of neighbors to give help in time of trouble is especially stressed. If a man's house burns down, as houses sometimes do, his neighbors should hurry to help to rescue his family and goods, and they should assist him to build a new house. The Nyoro alarm call is a loud ululation, the sound of which carries a long way, and all able-bodied men should respond to it. Failure to do so would be unneighborly; today it is an offense punishable in the chiefs' courts. It is good that neighbors should meet together often and talk about village affairs, and mutual visiting is common. A guest is always politely received, and he should be offered food and drink if the householders themselves are at a meal. It is bad manners to refuse such an invitation, for it suggests that you suspect your host of being a sorcerer, who wishes to poison you.

Eating and drinking together express the friendly relations which should subsist between neighbors. It is thought to be a bad thing for a man to eat alone; Nyoro say that in the old days a man could be "fined" by an informal court of neighbors if he persisted in eating by himself. Communal beer drinking, especially, is a means of emphasizing and affirming village solidarity, and beer parties are common. People come together to feast and drink beer on various occasions, some of which are explicitly concerned with the maintenance of social solidarity or its restoration when it has been disrupted. Nyoro also drink beer for no other reason than that it is available and that it is agreeable to drink. Formerly, anybody would have joined in a beer party without payment; nowadays a small profit may be made by the retail sale of a part of the brew to anyone who wants and can afford it. But even today, where the brew is a small one and the guests are a few close friends and neighbors, no charge is made.

The beer now usually drunk is made from a special variety of banana. The fruit is cooked for some hours in an underground earth oven, then peeled, mixed with a sweet-smelling species of grass, some water added, and the mixture trodden out in a prepared hollow in the ground which is lined with segments of banana stems. The treading out of the beer is itself a social occasion; neighbors sit around talking in the shade of the banana trees while the beer is being prepared, sometimes drinking a glass of the sweet unfermented juice. This liquid is then decanted into a large wooden trough which may hold up to twenty gallons, some grain is put in to hasten fermentation, and the brew is covered over and left for three days. On the fourth day it is ready for drinking. Quite a lot of beer has to be brewed at once (it would not be worth the trouble involved to prepare only a small amount), and the beer will not keep for more than a day or so. This means that beer drinking is bound to be a social occasion, since one man and his family cannot consume a whole brew, and it also means that all the beer brewed must be drunk at one sitting. Thus beer parties usually start early in the morning, and they continue for as long as the beer lasts, rarely later than the early afternoon. They usually take place in the open, often in the shady banana grove where the beer was brewed. Most guests sit on the ground, or on handy logs or wisps of dry grass, but senior or especially respected men are sometimes given European-style chairs or stools to sit on. In former times women did not attend beer parties; now they often do, but a married man would be angry if his wife went to a beer party otherwise than in his company or with his permission, and domestic quarrels sometimes arise from this cause. Women usually sit in a group by themselves a few yards apart from the men, though even this degree of segregation is now breaking down, and especially in the beer shops near the town the sexes mingle promiscuously.

At every beer party there is a formal "host." He selects another man, usually a member of his own household but perhaps a friend of lower status than himself, to dispense the beer, which is brought in to the center of the party in a large earthenware pot containing several gallons. From this it is ladled into the gourd drinking vessels (or nowadays often the enamel mugs or glasses) of the guests. There is a strict order of priority; after the host has tasted the beer, it is first given to the more important people present, and lesser guests may have to wait a long time for their turn. If the host (or, where the beer is for sale, any person who can afford it) wishes to compliment somebody, he may present him with a gourd containing up to a gallon or more, or even a whole pot. Such a gesture is greeted with clapping and shouts of satisfaction by all present, even by those least likely to profit by it. The recipient is under no obligation to drink all or even any of his gift himself; it is now his, and he should in any case give a good deal of it away to his own intimates.

If there is only a little beer, the drinkers may sit around in groups and talk about the topics of the moment for as long as the beer lasts. But if there is enough beer, before long somebody is certain to fetch a drum, and dancing and singing begin in a cleared space in the middle of the group of drinkers, who sing and clap their hands in rhythm with the dancing. One or at most two individuals dance at a time, and the dancing and songs often have an implicitly or explicitly sexual reference. The movements of the dancers' hips are often emphasized by a cloth or even a folded jacket tied around the waist. Nowadays women sometimes join in the dance, which they perform in the same manner as the men. After each dance everybody cheers and thanks the performer, and shakes his hand. The party continues for as long as the beer lasts; people then gradually drift away. It is unusual in rural Bunyoro for serious quarrels or fights to break out at beer parties where all the drinkers are near neighbors, though sometimes they do. Communal beer drinking is traditionally regarded as a good thing (though constant drunkenness is not), and although a man who spends all his time at beer parties is despised, one who never drinks beer with his neighbors is regarded as an eccentric or worse.

Most of the occasions on which people come together to drink beer conform to this general pattern. But as well as the informal beer drinks which take place simply because the beer is there, there are also more formal occasions when neighbors and kinsmen should drink beer together and, sometimes, eat together as well. We go on to note some of these occasions, bearing in mind the traditional part that drinking plays in bringing people together in close and friendly relationship.

In addition to the informal kind of drinking party which has just been described, there is in Bunyoro a traditional custom of bringing a gift of food and drink to a friend's house as a gesture of friendship and regard. This is usually rather more than simply a transaction between two individuals. On the day appointed, the bringer of the gifts (if he is a man) comes accompanied by his wife and members of his household, together with a number of his friends and neighbors. The person who is to receive the gifts has also assembled a number of his kinsmen and neighbors in his house, and has laid in a stock of food and drink. They have a party, and the combined stocks of food and beer are consumed amid great singing, dancing, and rejoicing. Anybody may "feast" another in this way, except that a man may not "feast" a woman, since it is for women to serve and make food for men, not vice versa. But it is particularly appropriate between men who are associated by a blood pact, between a girl and a young man whom she hopes to marry, between a family and a man who stands in the relation of "son-in-law" to it, and between a group of neighbors and one of their number who has returned from a long journey. A young girl may also take a feast to the homestead where her older sister is married, partly in the hope of receiving a return present of money or clothes. For reciprocity is involved; the person or household which is feasted must itself contribute to the feast by providing food, beer, and perhaps a goat, and should also, nowadays, make a money present to the person who has brought the gifts. This money is divided among the gift-bringing party. Nyoro have a special word for this making of a return present, and such a return should be made by anyone who receives a gift. The return gift should bear some proportion to the gift given, but the correspondence should not be exact; a return gift of identical value with that given would offend, for it would suggest that this transaction was a purchase and not a friendly interchange of gifts, and it would imply that the receiver did not wish to continue the friendly relationship initiated by the first gift. Though the institution of "feasting" another person or family is now declining, Nyoro still value it highly. It expresses vividly the kind of relations which, Nyoro feel, ought to subsist between neighbors: it is a good thing for people who live near to one another to make feasts for one another from time to time.

Beer drinking and feasting in Bunyoro are also associated, as they are in other cultures, with what have been called "rites of passage"—ceremonial occasions when members of the community undergo important changes of status. The most obvious and important of these are birth, marriage, and death, and feasts are associated with each of these three events in Bunyoro. Some time after a child is born there is a small ceremony called "taking out the child," in which the infant is taken out of the house for the first time and placed on a mat where everybody can see it. The child is then named, usually though not necessarily by a patrilineal relative, a father or grandfather. There follows a small feast, which is usually attended by members of the household and a few relatives and neighbors. A goat may be killed, beer is drunk, and some small presents, nowadays usually a few cents, are given for the child. This is not a major occasion for feasting, and the party is mostly a family one. It lasts only for one day.

We have spoken already of the marriage feast, which is held when the bride ceremonially enters her husband's home. For Nyoro this is the greatest feast of all; it is attended by crowds of people, enormous quantities of beer, meat, and other food are consumed, and the party should continue for three or four days. At the same time a smaller but still considerable party is taking place at the home of the bride's parents (who are not allowed to attend the main feast). There beer specially provided for them by the bridegroom's family, called "the beer that comforts," is being drunk. Meat is also being eaten; the bridal party, then at the bridegroom's home, are expected to send home to the bride's parents at least one hind leg of a large goat which has been given to them by the bridegroom's father. Some months after the marriage the wife's mother, and a party from her home, should pay a formal visit to the newly married couple's house. This occasion is also marked by a feast, to which both groups contribute. Meat and beer are consumed, and there is much singing and dancing, though of course the wife's mother and her son-in-law may not meet face to face or address one another directly. In the old days, it is said, this feast used to continue for two or three days; nowadays the custom has almost died out.

Feasting is also associated with mortuary ceremonies. When a person dies, the members of the deceased's household may not prepare food or indeed do any kind of work for some days after the death. The interval is four days for a man's death, three for a woman's; four is associated with masculinity, three with femininity, in many cultural contexts in Bunyoro. Food is provided by neighbors for the bereaved. They may not wash, shave, or put on clean clothes during this period. On the third or fourth day relatives, friends, and neighbors gather at the deceased's house to eat and drink the food and beer that have been brought to "comfort" the bereaved. Burial takes place as soon as possible after death, except in the case of a household head, whose body should lie in his house for one night. At the mortuary feast for the head of a family a date is decided upon for the inheritance ceremony, which also entails a feast. This ceremony involves the formal installation of the heir in his father's place, the presentation to him of his father's spear and stick, and a good deal of speech making in the course of which the heir's new duties and responsibilities as head of the family are impressed upon him. After this, food and beer are consumed by the members of the household together with the relatives, friends, and neighbors present.

Feasting in Bunyoro is also associated with traditional religious ceremonies, of which the most important are concerned with the spirit possession cult and with sacrifice to the ancestral ghosts. These topics are considered in the next chapter; here I record merely that they, too, were occasions on which communal or group solidarity was manifested in ceremonial eating and drinking. Although the spirit possession cult is now largely an individual affair, it was formerly concerned with the well-being of extended family or lineage groups. Membership in the cult involves a lengthy process of initiation, at the end of which a feast is held. This feast is attended not only by all the local members of the cult group, but also by uninitiated friends, relatives, and neighbors of the new initiate. Though such feasts are now rarely held, Nyoro speak of them as having been among the most important of communal feasts, ranking with marriage feasts, with which they are often compared. The essentially religious nature of the spirit-cult feasts is stressed. Only certain kinds of food can be eaten at them; there should be meat, beer, and millet porridge, but "low status" vegetables such as beans, sweet potatoes, and cassava are not used. Included in the meal is a species of white fungus: the color white is important because the occasion is essentially one of "purifying" the house and its inhabitants, and in Nyoro culture (as in many others) the notions of whiteness and of purity are associated. The other ritual occasion for feasting is less important; traditionally, groups of closely related patrilineal kinsmen would meet together from time to time to sacrifice and to pay respect to the ghosts of the dead fathers of their lineage, and the accompanying ceremonies would include a shared meal. Strictly speaking, only kinsmen were concerned, but as with almost all Nyoro feasts and ceremonies any neighbor who happened to be present could attend.

There are other, lesser occasions upon which feasts may be held, such as the birth of twins, the successful conclusion of a hunt, or the occupation of a new house. But one major occasion for communal drinking and eating remains to be discussed, and that is when a dispute between villagers has been settled by an informal tribunal of local people. This is one of Bunyoro's most important communal institutions, and I discuss it in the context of the inter-individual frictions and disputes in the settlement of which it traditionally played (and still plays) an essential part.

Disputes and Their Settlement

Although social relations in a Nyoro village community are on the whole strikingly easy and friendly, rules are bound to be broken sometimes and interests to conflict, and disputes and disagreements inevitably occur. Often trouble arises over property; petty thefts take place; debts remain unpaid; brothers sometimes quarrel after their father's death about the disposal of goods or livestock. Men sometimes quarrel about, and with, women; accusations of adultery are made; husbands and wives accuse one another of cruelty or neglect, and one or other wishes for divorce. There may be arguments about the custody or the paternity of children. People sometimes abuse or slander one another, and perhaps even accuse one another of sorcery; young men may be disrespectful to their fathers or to other senior people toward whom they should behave with propriety. Men may quarrel over cultivation rights, or trespass by stock. All these issues, and many more, may lead to disputes which are too serious to be settled simply by the parties themselves.

Nyoro culture provides various means of expressing the antagonisms which arise in these several ways. Sometimes people resort to violence, but this is on the whole unusual in Bunyoro. Hostility is more likely to be expressed in mutual recrimination and personal abuse, in which threats of sorcery may play a part. More seriously, it may express itself in the imputation and perhaps the actual practice of sorcery (I leave this for discussion in the next chapter). It may also find expression in the destruction of property, typically in arson. The old-fashioned type of house—roofed, and sometimes walled as well, with dried grass—is highly inflammable, and it is easy for a man to thrust a lighted brand into an enemy's thatch and get safely away before the alarm is raised.

Certain grave criminal offenses such as homicide, rape, or robbery are nowadays the concern of the Uganda Protectorate police force, which is responsible for the apprehension and prosecution of criminals. But in rural areas the police count on the help of the local authorities. Such serious cases are tried in the first instance in the district commissioners' or the resident magistrates' courts. Cases involving Europeans, or civil cases between Africans where the property in dispute is valued above a certain limit, are also heard in the European courts. But lesser disputes or offenses involving neighbors may be dealt with in one of two ways. The case may be taken to the nearest official native court of first instance for hearing; these are the subchiefs' courts, established by Protectorate legislation and having powers to fine, imprison, and award compensation. A litigant dissatisfied with the decision of such a court may appeal to the court next above (the county chief's court), and thence, through the district court, to the High Court of the Protectorate. But, as in other African societies, disputes within a Nyoro community may, if they are not very serious, be dealt with by an informal local tribunal or "court" of neighbors, which I call a "neighborhood court." They *should* in fact be so dealt with in the first place, and when a minor dispute is brought before a chief he may ask whether an attempt has been made to settle it at the neighborhood level. If no such attempt has been made, he is quite likely to send the intending litigants away. In the remainder of this chapter we shall be concerned with these local tribunals, which strikingly express the social values basic in Nyoro community life.

A neighborhood court consists simply of a group of neighbors gathered together quite informally to adjudicate upon a matter in dispute. It only comes into being when somebody makes it known that he has a complaint against somebody else and wishes to have the matter dealt with in this way. In such a case a few neighbors experienced in arbitration, or with particular knowledge of the matter in issue, may be invited to attend, but any neighbor may drop in without invitation, provided that he is a householder in good standing and a reputable person. These courts are not clan or lineage tribunals: there are some kinds of disputes which are mainly the concern of kin, such as quarrels about inheritance, but as a rule the basis of representation is neighborhood as much as, sometimes more than, any kind of kinship link. Whether the dispute is between kin or unrelated persons the basic pattern is always the same, though the proportional representation may vary; in either case kinsmen of the parties may be present, and so also may neighbors who are kinsmen of neither.

After the parties to the dispute have stated their cases and the witnesses, if there are any, have been heard, the assembled neighbors discuss the issues raised and usually reach a unanimous decision. They then direct the person who has been found to be at fault to bring beer and meat to the injured party's house on a specified day and time. If the person charged accepts the tribunal's decision, he does this in due course, and there follows a feast, in which both the parties, and the neighbors who adjudicated on the case, take part. After this the dispute is supposed to be finished, and it should not be referred to again. The following is an example of a case settled in this manner:

At a beer party a middle-aged man, Yonasani, was drunk and insulted a youth called Tomasi. Tomasi wanted to fight with Yonasani, but was prevented from doing so by his companions. However, he left the party early, and lay in wait for Yonasani on the path to the latter's house. As Yonasani passed he hit him on the head with a stick, knocking him down, and fled. But Yonasani suspected who had attacked him, and the next day he complained to Tomasi's father. When Tomasi was accused, he denied all knowledge of the affair, but on Yonasani's threatening to take the case to the chief's court Tomasi's father said that he and his son would agree to have the case settled in a neighborhood court. About half-a-dozen neighbors were accordingly summoned to adjudicate on the matter, and they met at Tomasi's house. After everybody had spoken, the neighbors discussed the case briefly, and they all agreed that Tomasi had hit Yonasani, and that he had been wrong to do so, for if he had a complaint against Yonasani he should have taken it before a neighborhood court. The court accordingly ordered Tomasi to bring four large jars of beer and five shillings worth of meat to Yonasani's house about a week later. He agreed to do this, and on the appointed day all the people who had attended the hearing were present, as well as Tomasi and Yonasani and the members of their households. Tomasi was told to serve the beer, and to choose a friend to roast the meat. Then, in the words of an informant who was at the party, "We began to eat and drink, and everyone started to joke and laugh, as they do at a wedding feast. Soon some people began dancing, and we accompanied them by singing and clapping our hands. By now Tomasi and Yonasani had become quite friendly with each other as they used to be before they quarrelled. And from that day to this the quarrel between them has been finished."

The case of Yonasani and Tomasi exhibits the characteristic features of this kind of settlement. The initial action is taken by the complainant, not by the court, which of course does not exist until it is summoned. A penalty is always imposed, and this penalty is always the same, a payment of beer and meat which are to be consumed in a joint feast by all the parties to the case. Although Yonasani's case might have been taken directly to the chief's court for settlement, it was not, since the complainant had expressed himself willing to have it heard in the village. This last point is important; Nyoro villagers consider it unneighborly to take a minor case to the chief's court, or, as they would put it, "to the Government" (opposing in this as in other contexts the superimposed state to the local community), and it shows kindness and forbearance on the part of a complainant not to do so. To permit the case to be heard among neighbors and friends implies that the offender is still accepted as a member of the community; to send the case for hearing by "strangers" in the chief's court, where heavier penalties such as imprisonment may be imposed, would suggest that his own community rejected him.

The neighborhood court aims if possible to reconcile the parties to the dispute—at any rate to reach a compromise which they will accept. The institution expresses the high value which Nyoro attach to good relations between neighbors, and its most important function is to restore village harmony when this has been breached, by reintegrating the delinquent into his community. Of course neighborhood courts do not always succeed in achieving complete, or indeed any, agreement between the parties; it would be astonishing if they did. Sometimes no solution is reached, and sometimes one party is dissatisfied and refuses to accept the court's decision, preferring to have recourse to the more powerful sanctions of the chiefs' courts. But in the great majority of cases a satisfactory settlement is reached at village level.

It is plain that the primary aim of these village tribunals is the restoration of good relations, not the punishment of an offender. It is true that meat and beer cost money, but the order to provide them is not imposed simply to inflict hardship on the delinquent. If one suggests that the culprit suffers by being penalized in this way, Nyoro point out that he enjoys—or should enjoy —the feast just as much as the other people present do. Indeed he is the formal host, and the position of host is an honorable one. Thus he is really being paid a compliment, and the community is reasserting its confidence in him. The beer and meat are not a "fine", for their purpose is to rehabilitate rather than to punish. If it ever should happen that the traditional payment in kind is commuted to a payment in cash (there is luckily no sign of this happening as yet), it is obvious that the neighborhood courts will completely change their character. First of all, a money payment would inevitably sooner or later find its way into the pockets of the powerful or less scrupulous; secondly, hard cash cannot be eaten or drunk, and it is the communal feasts that are their proper conclusion that give these informal courts their great social importance. We have seen that feasting together is the most important way of manifesting and reasserting social solidarity and good-neighborly relations. It is by this means, too, that breaches of such good relations are traditionally repaired, errant individuals reintegrated into village society, and the most vital community values themselves reaffirmed.

7

The Supernatural

IN THE CONDITIONS of most simple societies everyone has frequent and direct experience of illness and death, but there is still little or no understanding of the physical causes of these events. Thus in rural Bunyoro illness is common and often fatal, the rate of infant mortality is high, and hospital facilities, though they exist, are few and far between. One has to live for a period in the primitive conditions to which many of the less advanced peoples are accustomed, far from Western medical aid, in order to realize how powerless one can feel when illness attacks or threatens. A Westerner in such circumstances feels that there is nothing much he can do: he probably inclines to fatalism and hopes for the best. But for a member of the simpler culture there is much that he can do; his culture provides ways of dealing with such situations which are socially and psychologically, if not clinically, satisfying. Thus Nyoro, like other people, have beliefs in what we would call supernatural agents, and it is believed that these may be propitiated by sacrifice and prayer, or made use of by certain magical techniques. The slow decline of witchcraft beliefs in Western countries shows how tenacious such systems of thought and the patterns of behavior based on them may be. Often they survive, perhaps adapting themselves in the process, into times very different from those with which they were traditionally associated. We shall see that this has happened in Bunyoro.

Supernatural beliefs and practices, then, may be in some degree understood as providing acceptable explanations for events which would otherwise be inexplicable, and so relieving ignorance and doubt. But they are more than just a body of beliefs; most important of all, they provide a means of coping with events. To act is better than to remain inert in the face of actual or threatened misfortune, and where the victim cannot refer to a body of empirical knowledge for help, then magical and ritual procedures, which are not ordinarily subject to empirical testing in the same way as practical techniques, may provide a socially acceptable recipe for action. Even though these activities do not (we suppose) bring about the ends they aim at, at least they make the performer feel that he is dealing effectively with the situation, and so relieve his anxiety. And there is always some kind of internal consistency about such systems of magical beliefs, so that failure, when it occurs, is generally explicable in terms of the system itself.

Education is advancing in Bunyoro, but most peasants still cling to the traditional magical practices, even though administrators and missionaries have actively discouraged them for over fifty years, and some of them have been made into criminal offenses punishable in the courts. We shall see that in certain cases Nyoro have even adapted their ancient ritual, without altering its essential character, to the changed circumstances of today.

People usually seek magical help in situations of misfortune; if everything were for the best in the best of all possible worlds, there would be no need for magic. The commonest kind of misfortune is, of course, illness, either one's own or that of a person for whom one is responsible, such as a child or another member of the family. The first thing to be done is to discover the cause of the illness, and to do this it is necessary to consult a diviner. Diviners may be consulted, however, for other reasons besides illness. A man may hate another, and wish to injure him, and he may want to know the best kind of magic medicine or technique to employ. Women may be childless, and wish to discover what it is that is preventing them from having children. A woman may believe that her husband has lost interest in her, especially if he has just procured a second wife or is talking of obtaining one, and she may wish to know how to recover his affection. A man may want to discover the identity of a thief or an incendiarist, or at least to bring down punishment on such a person even though he remain unknown. In Bunyoro, problems of these and many other kinds are brought to the diviners, and the diviners provide what are on the whole acceptable answers.

In Bunyoro most diviners work part time; they are usually subsistence farmers like everyone else, and they are not held in any particular regard except when they are actually divining. But a few people have made big reputations as doctors and diviners, and these often travel long distances to practice, and may make large profits. Most diviners are "doctors" as well; in addition to diagnosing the cause of the trouble they may also provide a cure. In other cases a diviner may pass a patient on to another doctor who specializes in the treatment of the particular kind of affliction which has been diagnosed. Simple divination by an ordinary part-time diviner is not very expensive; the cost varies from about fifty cents to a few shillings. The treatment of some kinds of ailments, however (for example, those requiring initiation into one of the several spirit-possession cults), or the procuring of medicine to kill an enemy, may cost several pounds. The fee depends both on the kind of treatment needed and on the fame of the practitioner who is consulted.

There are many different ways of divining, but by far the commonest nowadays is by the use of cowry shells. These small seashells, which were formerly used as currency in many parts of Africa, have their convex sides leveled off, so that when they are thrown on the ground there are equal chances of their falling with their natural cleft or their leveled side up. Nine are used for divination (nine is a ritually auspicious number in many contexts). When a man goes to consult a diviner, they both sit on the ground facing each other, with a goat skin spread out on the ground between them. The client describes the symptoms to the diviner and puts some money "for the shells" in the small bowl placed on the mat for the purpose. The diviner then holds his handful of cowries to his mouth and says "thus my forefathers divined before me; this is true divination and not deception." He also entreats the shells to divine well. He then scatters the handful of shells on the mat several times, and in due course, partly according to the way the shells fall and partly according to his own independent interpretation, he identifies his client's trouble, and says whether he can do anything to help him. It is difficult to know how far the diagnosis is conventionally conditioned by the way the shells fall at each throw, and how far the diviner is free to diagnose as he thinks fit. There are certain patterns which everyone knows how to interpret: if the shells fall with the cut-off side down the prognosis is bad, if the other way up it is good; if one shell comes to rest on top of another a death is imminent; if the shells scatter widely a journey is prognosticated; three or more in a straight line mean a safe return; and so on. But my impression is that although there are some conventions of this kind, in this and other divining techniques it is preeminently up to the diviner to make his own interpretation, which he ordinarily does in the light of his local knowledge of the case, and of his client's unintended revelations of the circumstances.

If the diviner diagnoses sorcery, as he is quite likely to do, he hands the cowries to his client to throw. Before the client throws them he whispers to them inaudibly the name of a suspect. After seeing how the shells have fallen, the diviner says whether or not the person named is the culprit. The throw may be repeated several times before a positive decision is reached (it may not be reached at all), and often a client tests the diviner by naming people whom he is quite sure are innocent before naming people he really suspects. To accuse anyone of sorcery is a serious matter, and most diviners are careful never themselves to name a particular person as a sorcerer or even to indicate him in unambiguous terms. The diviner simply says that his shells confirm what the client has himself suggested, or else he indicates the sorcerer in vague terms ("a tall dark man living to the north") which the client himself applies to the person he suspects. If the consultation reveals the identity of the guilty person, the client may, if he wishes to make quite sure, go to one or more other diviners to confirm or correct a first opinion. If he is satisfied, he may ask the diviner what he should do. The diviner may then sell him an antidote to the medicine which has been used against him, or provide him with the recipe for medicine to kill the sorcerer, or, sometimes, send him to another practitioner who is more skilled in dealing with the kind of sorcery diagnosed.

But other troubles besides sorcery may be diagnosed (though this is probably the commonest), and there are other techniques besides the throwing of cowry shells (though this is the most usual). Other oracular techniques are the throwing on a mat of nine small squares of leather, the ensuing patterns being studied as in the case of the cowry oracle, and the sprinkling on water of the ashes of the burnt leaves of certain species of plants, the forms the ash assumes being interpreted by the diviner. There is also a rubbing oracle, a short stick which the diviner smears with the blood of a slaughtered goat and rubs up and down with his fingers; this oracle gives its decisions by causing the manipulator's fingers to stick at certain points. Like the ancient Greeks, Nyoro also practice divination by examining the entrails of animals and birds, especially fowl; from certain signs in the internal organs a diviner can determine whether his client will recover. It is said that in ancient times cattle were sometimes used for this purpose; such a case occurs in the Nyoro myth recounted in Chapter 2. Of considerable importance even today is divination by means of spirit possession; it is believed that through their living mediums certain powerful spirits may answer questions put to them by clients.

I have said that, in Bunyoro, illness or other misfortune is often attributed to sorcery. It may, also, be thought to be due to ancestral or other ghosts, or to the activity of certain other powerful nonhuman spirits. We now consider in more detail the content and contexts of these three different kinds of responses.

The Nyoro word which I translate "sorcery" means to injure another person by the secret use of harmful medicines or techniques. These usually (though not essentially) involve what we should call a magical or nonempirical element. They generally have a symbolic or "expressive" quality, and they are not usually tested and varied experimentally as practical techniques are. Thus for Nyoro it is sorcery to make a medicine out of bits of hair, nail parings, and other parts of a certain person's body, to put this medicine in an animal horn, and to place the horn in the roof of that person's house with intent to injure him. But it is also sorcery to obtain a deadly medicine from an expert and to place it in an enemy's food or drink. Even to set a man's house on fire at dead of night in the hope of destroying him and his family is a kind of sorcery. These illustrations afford another example of the danger of uncritically applying the vocabulary of Western culture to other people's ways of thought: for Nyoro, sorcery implies secret and harmful activity, usually carried out under cover of darkness, and although it usually implies what we should call magical procedure it need not do so. An informant put the matter clearly when he said,

A sorcerer is a person who wants to kill people. He may do it by blowing medicine toward them, or by putting it in the victim's food or water, or by hiding it in the path where he must pass. People practice sorcery against those whom they hate. They practice it against those who steal from them, and also against people who are richer than they are. Sorcery is brought about by envy, hatred, and quarreling.

We saw in Chapter 6 that sorcery and imputations of it provide one of the commonest ways in which interpersonal conflicts, when they do occur, express themselves in Bunyoro. If a man becomes ill, or if one of his children sickens and dies, and it is known that he was on bad terms with somebody, that person is likely to be suspected, especially if they have recently quarreled. There are certain phrases, such as "you'll see me!," which are often, *post hoc,* construed as threats of sorcery, and which may even be used as such.

Since sorcery expresses interpersonal antagonisms, it is not usually thought of as acting at a distance; if there is no personal contact then there can be no occasion for its use. As we should expect, it occurs and is suspected most often in those social relationships where there is social strain. Thus women often accuse their co-wives of sorcery, and husbands their wives. Men sometimes accuse their brothers of sorcery; we noted in Chapter 5 that jealousy between brothers is not unusual. Unrelated persons may also engage in sorcery because of some dispute, or because one of them resents the wealth or eminence of the other; thus rich people are supposed to be especially susceptible. There are men and women who are likely suspects because of their surly or unsociable dispositions; such people may in the course of time build up reputations as sorcerers. The following is an example of a sorcery situation:

Yowana bought a piece of timber to make a door with, but it was stolen before he could use it. After searching the village he found it in the house of a neighbor, Isoke. He accused Isoke of stealing it, but since Isoke denied the theft and there were no witnesses, the charge failed. A few days later Yowana's house was burned down and he lost all his property. He did not know who had done this (though he suspected Isoke), so, informants afterwards said, he obtained from a vendor of powerful medicines a substance which if smeared on those of the posts of the burned house which remained standing would cause the incendiarist to suffer from dysentery and burning pains in his chest. Yowana is said to have applied the medicine as directed, and four days later Isoke became ill. His brothers consulted the local diviners, who said that Yowana's medicine was the cause of the illness. Isoke then summoned Yowana, confessed to him that he had burned his house and also that he had stolen the timber, and promised to make restitution. Isoke's brothers begged Yowana to get an antidote from the vendor of the original medicine, so that Isoke might be cured. Yowana promised to do so, but unfortunately Isoke died. In this case complaints were made to the Protectorate police and Yowana was arrested for suspected murder, but an autopsy on Isoke's body showed no signs of poisoning, and Yowana was released. Nonetheless, nobody doubted that Yowana had killed Isoke by sorcery, least of all Yowana, who was heard to boast at beer parties of his prowess.

Many other cases could be quoted to show how easily interpersonal disputes of all kinds can turn into sorcery accusations. If one man hates another he will wish to injure him, and it may be supposed that if he has the knowledge or can afford to pay for it he will use one or another of the numerous techniques of sorcery to achieve his end. He may in any case be tempted, when his feelings are aroused, to utter threats which may give him the best of the argument by terrifying his opponent, but which may afterwards be interpreted as threats of sorcery.

There are several alternatives open to a victim when sorcery has been diagnosed and the sorcerer identified. Where the sufferer knows that he has wronged the sorcerer (as in the case just quoted) he may acknowledge his fault and beg him for an antidote. He may, if the illness is not grave, be treated for it by the diviner-practitioner. He may turn the same weapon on his attacker, using a more powerful medicine to injure him. Or he may, if all else fails, retaliate with physical violence; a considerable proportion of Bunyoro's few homicides arise in this way. He may, finally, bring an accusation of sorcery before the local chief; this would usually happen in the case of persons believed to be habitual sorcerers, who have become a serious public menace. In pre-European times such persons, if convicted, were tied up in dried banana leaves (which are very inflammable) and burnt; nowadays they are tried in the chiefs' courts and if found guilty may be sentenced to a term of imprisonment. On their release, public opinion may force them to move to another village where they are not known.

The modern courts are not authorized to convict people of being sorcerers or witches, for these crimes are not recognized by the European government. But it is a statutory offense to "hold oneself out to be" a sorcerer or a witch, and the distinction between this and actually being one is less clear to Nyoro than it is to European legislators. And it is plain from the evidence given in court cases that there are people who do practice sorcery. Men have been caught in the act of placing magic medicines in the thatch of people's houses, and when the homes of accused persons are searched, as they usually are, recognized implements of sorcery such as animal horns, bones, and various medicines are very often found. Accused persons often admit their guilt: to do so may incur conviction, but it may also greatly enhance the respect and fear in which an otherwise inconsiderable person is held.

Like other African peoples, Nyoro say that sorcery is more common now than it was in the past, and they attribute this to the very much milder penalties now imposed. But we may suppose that the increase, so far as it exists, rather reflects the increase in interpersonal tensions and the growth of individualism which are involved in the breakdown of many of the traditional standards and sanctions. Certainly sorcery beliefs and the associated techniques are still widespread in Bunyoro. And, anachronistic though they are in the "modern" African society into which Bunyoro is slowly developing, there is no doubt that they are still effective sanctions for conformity to approved norms. Nyoro villagers know that unneighborly behavior may arouse the enmity of others, and they believe that such enmity may be expressed through sorcery, probably with serious consequences. Equally, the unsociable or bad-tempered person may bring down on himself accusations of sorcery, and although the penalties for this are less severe than the traditional ones, they may still serve to discourage (though not to eliminate) certain kinds of socially disapproved behavior.

For Nyoro, misfortune may be due to the action of ghosts and of other kinds of spirits, as well as to sorcery. A ghost is the disembodied spirit of a dead person. When a person is alive this vital principle has another name, which we may translate "soul," and it is thought of as inhabiting the breast.

Ghosts are never seen, though they may manifest themselves in dreams; they are thought of rather as immaterial forces diffused through space. They are associated with the underworld, and with the color black. On the whole they are maleficent, and Nyoro say that when people die they cease to think of their living relatives as "theirs." By this they mean that ghosts no longer acknowledge the ties of affection and obligation which they felt when they were alive. It is natural that ghosts should be thought of as on the whole ill-disposed toward the living, for it is only when illness or some other misfortune takes one to the diviner that ghosts, like sorcerers, become socially relevant.

If ghostly activity is diagnosed as the cause of misfortune, the agent is most likely to be the ghost of somebody who has been wronged or neglected by the "victim" and who has died with a grudge against him. Most ghosts are therefore those of deceased relatives, for, as we have seen, every Nyoro is bound to many different kinds of relatives and affines in a network of mutual obligations which should not be neglected. Where particular obligations are stressed, as between sons and fathers, sisters' sons and their mothers' brothers (a sister's son's ghost is specially feared), and brothers, so that a breach of these obligations is particularly serious, ghostly activity is often diagnosed. Few people can be sure that they have not at some time neglected or offended some relative who has since died. Even the ghosts of distant relatives, or of unrelated persons, may be responsible for illness. In former times the ghosts of war captives or domestic slaves were particularly feared—another example of the way in which a culture sometimes invests with ritual power people who occupy positions of social subordination. So, like sorcery beliefs, fear of ghostly vengeance may be a sanction for good interpersonal relations; bad behavior may lead not only to reprisals by the living through sorcery, it may lead also to reprisals by the dead through ghostly activity.

Here is a typical case in which illness was explained by reference to the activity of ghosts:

> Yozefu's small daughter became ill, and shortly afterwards the son of Yozefu's full brother Yowana became sick too. The diviners were consulted, and it was found that the cause of these illnesses was Yowana's ill treatment of his father, who had died some months previously. Just before his death, Yowana had forcibly dissuaded his (Yowana's) wife from preparing food for him, on the ground that he had his own wife to take care of him. This had angered the old man; he had died without being reconciled to his son, and it was his ghost which was causing the children's illness. When this was discovered the ghost was enabled to say what it wanted through a possession ceremony, a shrine was built and a sacrifice was made, and eventually the sick children recovered.

The above example of Yozefu and Yowana shows that ghostly vengeance often attacks not the offender himself, but his (or even his brother's) children. A man is most vulnerable through his children, for not only will posterity remember him through them, but also after his death they will provide his ghost with the attentions it needs. Nyoro can hardly be described as ancestor worshippers, but the ghosts of the father and the father's father are nonetheless regarded as important, and sacrifices and other attentions should be given to them from time to time. Such sacrifices provide one of the occasions for feasting which was referred to in Chapter 6.

When ghostly affliction is diagnosed, two kinds of action can be taken. If the ghost is an important one, such as that of a near relative, it must be induced to "possess" the victim or someone who represents him, and through him or her to say what has offended it and what it wishes to be done. Nobody can be posssesed by the ghost of a dead person until he has undergone a lengthy initiation into the spirit possession cult, some account of which is given below. The directions given by a ghost usually include an instruction to build a small spirit hut or shrine for it; it may also demand the sacrifice of a goat. Ghosts conventionally express their resentment at neglect in terms of food; they say that they are hungry and want meat. Alternatively, the ghost may demand that a black goat be consecrated to it; such a goat may not be sold or slaughtered for secular purposes, but must be reserved in the homestead as the property of the ghost. Ghost shrines are small untidily made replicas of huts, cone shaped, and usually about eighteen inches high; in them are put the skull and some of the other bones of the sacrificed animal, together with certain other small ritually significant objects, such as a piece of a special kind of termite hill. If the ghost is an unimportant one, however—that of a stranger or a slave or a very remote relative, for instance—there is no need to enter in this way into an enduring relationship with it. It may be "caught" and destroyed by an expert who is skilled in such matters. When the offending ghost has possessed the victim or his representative, it may be induced to "leave the head" of its victim and to enter an ordinary earthenware pot. The pot is then quickly closed and, together with the enclosed ghost, it is disposed of either by burning it or by throwing it in an unfrequented part of the bush. I have been told that some practitioners place dried banana leaves in the pot and also imprison a small lizard in it: the rustling of the lizard in the leaves is then represented as being the ghost's struggles to escape.

I turn now to the third major class of "nonnatural" agents which may be held to be responsible for particular illnesses and other misfortunes: spirits or "powers." The cult of certain of these spirits is the traditional Nyoro religion. I spoke in Chapter 2 of the Chwezi, a wonderful race of people who are supposed to have come to Bunyoro many centuries ago, ruled the country for a brief period, and then vanished mysteriously. These people are said to have possessed amazing wisdom and skills, and to have left behind them a technique of spirit possession of which they themselves were the objects. We cannot now say whether there ever were such people, or whether, like the earliest Greek gods, they are partly or even wholly personifications of certain elemental natural forces. Certainly different Chwezi spirits are traditionally associated with particular natural features, such as thunder, rain, and so on. Also, they are thought and spoken of rather as things than as persons, and Nyoro clearly distinguish them from ghosts. There are said to be nineteen important Chwezi spirits, and in the traditional cult each one of the various localized agnatic groups into which Bunyoro is said to have been divided stood in a special relationship to one or other of these powers. Every such group had its initiated shaman or medium, who might be either a man or a woman, and on ceremonial occasions this medium would become possessed by the Chwezi spirit associated with his or her group; in this way the spirit would express its needs and wishes. These "tutelary" spirits were supposed to take care of the health, prosperity, and, especially, the fertility of all the members of the group, and these group possession ceremonies were occasions of great feasting and rejoicing. Even today, sterility and other afflictions are sometimes diagnosed by diviners as being due to the neglect of a household or group Chwezi spirit.

In recent times, however, the cult of spirit possession has become increasingly individualized. Even in traditional times the power responsible for a particular illness or misfortune could be a Chwezi spirit other than the one associated with the sufferer through his group membership. It could even be an alien, non-Chwezi power; some of these, immigrants from neighboring countries, have been known for a long time in Bunyoro. Nyoro distinguish between "white" and "black" spirits. The white ones are the group Chwezi whose influence on the local community, so long as they are not neglected, is supposed to be wholly beneficial; the black ones are all the non-Chwezi spirits. In recent years there has been an enormous increase in the variety of "black" spirits, and all informed Nyoro agree that the traditional group cult is declining at the expense of the more individualistic "black" cults. Among powers currently the objects of individualistic cults are various spirits supposed to have come from the Nilotic regions to the north of Bunyoro, as well as from other regions. Those powers which are directly or indirectly associated with Europeans are especially striking. These include such spirits as "Europeanness" (not, it should be noted, individual Europeans), "aeroplanes," and— peculiar perhaps to Bunyoro—a remarkable spirit called "Empolandi," or "Polishness." This last grew from the fact that during the last world war several hundred expatriate Poles spent some years in a large camp in northern Bunyoro. So large a number of white persons all in one place was something new, and more than a little ominous, to Nyoro, and the phenomenon was readily enough assimilated to the traditional mediumistic cult.

What is common to all the spirits or powers which we have discussed is that they express, or may originally have expressed, new, formidable, and potentially dangerous kinds of power. The spirit cult appears to afford an acceptable way of coming to terms with such phenomena, with which, at Bunyoro's present stage of cultural development, there is no other obvious way of dealing. Thus, for example, through the possession cult, a Nyoro peasant may come to some sort of terms with "European-ness" (as he conceives this abstraction), whereas it is less easy for him to make any sort of real contact with actual Europeans, important though he knows these remarkable people to be.

I spoke in Chapter 6 of the feasting traditionally associated with initiation into the possession cult. Initiations nowadays are smaller and necessarily clandestine affairs, for participation in the cult is now regarded as a criminal offense. But even today, whatever the spirit or power whose activity is diagnosed, the only way of dealing with it is by the formal initiation of the sufferer (or of an appropriate representative). Until this has been done the spirit cannot enter properly into the sufferer's head (though it may continue to afflict him in various ways), so that it can, through him, say what is needed to achieve a cure. Initiation is a long process. It involves the participation of a number of previously initiated mediums, and it may require the payment of a substantial fee, nowadays up to twenty pounds or more. In addition, the initiate and his family must provide large quantities of food and beer for the feast. I cannot here describe the complex rites involved in initiation, which culminate in the manifestation of symptoms of possession by the initiate and others, after a state of actual or simulated dissociation has been achieved through the rhythmic use of drums, gourd rattles, and singing. The ritual seems to express four main themes. First, it stresses the initiate's change of status; he ceases to be an ordinary person, as he was before. This change is dramatized in the ritual acting out of death and rebirth, in the bestowal on the initiate of certain cult objects, in certain food restrictions, and in the learning of a new Chwezi vocabulary. Second, there is a strong emphasis on secrecy; cult secrets may not be disclosed to noninitiates, and this is impressed on the novice by threats of physical violence and by formal cursing. Third, the initiate's new responsibilities to and his solidarity with his fellow mediums are emphasized, typically by the use between them of kinship and affinal terms. Finally, it is believed that initiation, like certain other major crises such as childbirth and death, puts the initiate into a state of grave ritual danger, which can only be relieved by the performance of specific ritual acts; in this case they include an act of ritual intercourse with a senior member of the cult.

Here I note only that spirit possession is the traditional Nyoro method of coping with dangerous spirits and powers, as well as with ghosts. As in the case of the beliefs and practices associated with sorcery, there is little reason to suppose that the incidence of the cult is declining; the chief effect of half a century's rigorous repression by both missionaries and Government has been to drive it underground. Indeed, the cult has shown a remarkable capacity to adapt to changed conditions. I suggested earlier in this chapter that where practical, "common-sense" techniques are lacking, or are inadequate to cope with the dangers and difficulties with which people are faced, magical and ritual remedies are usually resorted to. And we have seen that traditional Nyoro modes of religious thought have shown themselves well able to adapt to the new and unfamiliar forms of power associated with the coming of the Europeans. Nyoro have interpreted these manifestations of power as implying a proliferation of new kinds of spiritual entities, with which the preexisting possession cult is quite fitted to cope. It is a sign of the times that these new spirits are associated with the fortunes and misfortunes of individuals rather than of groups, with divination (for some "black" spirits can profit their mediums by divining), and sometimes even with sorcery, rather than with the traditional group cult.

8

Conclusion

IN CHAPTER 1 the point was raised whether it is reasonable to ask what Nyoro are really like. We can now try to answer that question, but we must first be clear as to what we are asking. The answer does not lie in merely assessing Nyoro temperament or character, which in any case I am not professionally qualified to do. As in most human populations, there are wide ranges in psychological type, and I have neither been particularly struck by nor attempted to establish the statistical preponderance of any one of them. As I said at the beginning of this book, by and large Nyoro are good-tempered, cooperative, intelligent, and tolerant; if there is some reserve and a touch of melancholy in their make-up this should not surprise anyone who is acquainted with Nyoro history. For the social anthropologist it is enough for all practical purposes to say that psychologically Nyoro are much the same as any other people, which is just what we should expect.

From the social point of view, on the other hand, it is possible to characterize Nyoro culture in individual terms, and to distinguish it from other cultures. This book has been written about the most important kinds of social relationships in which Nyoro participate, and we know that an essential part of any institutionalized social relationship is the way in which it is regarded by the people who participate in it. No social relationship can be made intelligible unless account is taken of the expectations, duties, and rights that it involves, and of the concepts and symbols by means of which the people who have it represent it to themselves. It is this ideological dimension of Nyoro social life that constitutes the sphere of Nyoro social values, and it is only by comprehending these (as far as we can) that we can hope to gain any real understanding of how Nyoro regard the world they live in. As Aristotle pointed out more than two thousand years ago, to be human is essentially to be social, and the world which Nyoro, like all other people, occupy is essentially a social world. In this book I have not only attempted to describe what Nyoro do (it would in any case be impossible to do this intelligibly without reference to what they think they do); I have also tried to show how they regard the various categories of persons who together make up their whole social environment. For almost all Nyoro the most important of these categories are the king and his relatives, the chiefs, the various kinds of kinsfolk and affines, the neighbors, and—not the least important—the Europeans who have in the past century so radically affected the social system, both directly and indirectly. I have said a good deal in the foregoing pages about Nyoro attitudes to all of these categories of persons, and in describing these attitudes I have at the same time been describing Nyoro social values.

I have remarked, also, in many contexts the degree to which, in recent years, many of these social values have been in conflict with one another. But this conflict is not new; it would be an illusion to suppose that in pre-European times Nyoro inhabited a sort of Golden Age, in which all values were in perfect harmony. We have seen that traditional Nyoro social structure exhibited a radical dichotomy between the "feudal," hierarchical state on the one hand, and the closely knit village community on the other. All Nyoro men had obligations in both contexts, and there is no doubt that these sometimes conflicted. But we may suppose that on the whole these conflicts were readily resoluble in terms of values which all Nyoro shared. Everybody acknowledged and accepted the hierarchical ordering of society, and (as we noted in an earlier chapter) throughout the social system roles were allocated on an ascriptive basis rather than on grounds of achievement. Whether a man was a chief or a peasant, it may be supposed that he found security and satisfaction in having a proper and recognized place both in the social hierarchy in which he enjoyed a definite status, and in the social groupings of family, kin, and neighborhood in each of which he was an accepted member. Even though state and community made different demands, these could on the whole be reconciled, for fundamentally similar attitudes to society and to the individual's place in it were implicit in both.

Western influence on the traditional organization has, on the other hand, been radical. We saw in Chapter 2 that its initial impact was violently disruptive of the old order, and over the years it has profoundly affected Nyoro attitudes and values at all levels. In the chapters which followed I indicated some of the main points of change. I stressed, too, that social change does not proceed evenly upon all fronts; traditional values and patterns of behavior sometimes coexist oddly—and uncomfortably—with modern ones in the same social situation. Thus many Nyoro still think of their Mukama as the traditional ritual and political head of the Nyoro kingdom, from whose personal favor all political authority should flow; yet at the same time most people recognize that for more than half a century he has been not the source but merely the instrument of political power. It is still sometimes thought that the chiefs, like the king, should be bound to their dependents by ties of personal acquaintanceship and mutual dependence; but it is increasingly being recognized that salaried, transferable chiefs cannot in the nature of the case maintain the old "feudal" relationships with the people they serve, and quite new kinds of expectations are growing up in regard to them. People still strongly feel that the king and his chiefs should provide constant feasts of meat and beer; at the same time the introduction of a cash economy has provided the peasant cultivators with new values and incentives which divert the products of their labor away from the chiefs into new and private channels. People still claim support and hospitality from their relatives and these claims are in principle admitted, but where a man's surplus energy goes into the growing of cash crops, or even into paid employment, and not into the production of food in excess of his immediate requirements, he cannot meet these claims. Clan and village solidarity are still highly valued, and Nyoro know that in the old days no man could live for himself alone; but they realize, too, that present-day conditions enable men to pursue their individual self-interest regardless of traditional obligations. Men still think that women should be subordinate, modest, and obedient, but they are forced to recognize that with increased economic independence they are increasingly claiming the same social independence as men, and are no longer as meek and obedient as they used to be. Nyoro say that money has made available many new and desirable things, but it has also brought new anxieties, for it has to be earned by the performance of new and not always congenial tasks if taxes, school fees, and other expenses are to be met.

There is, indeed, scarcely any aspect of Nyoro social life in which traditional and contemporary values are not, to some extent at least, at odds with one another. Nyoro are well aware that the economic and social conditions which Western contact has brought about have made many changes in the old pattern of political and community life, and the more traditionally minded disapprove of these changes. They say that their effect has been to lower the standards of morals and social behavior which prevailed in pre-European times. Old customs are dying out and old obligations are being neglected; the stress nowadays is no longer always on the group, but increasingly on the individual. When to these considerations are added Nyoro memories of military defeat and consequent subjection which, though fading, still survive, and their awareness of the rise of Ganda fortunes concomitantly with the decline of their own, it is understandable that old-fashioned Nyoro sometimes say (and they say it with resignation, not bitterness) that the Europeans have "spoiled" the country. It is understandable, too, that in this century Nyoro should have taken more pride in their past than in their present state, and that the charges of "apathy" and lack of enterprise sometimes leveled against them should have come, to some extent, to be reflected in Nyoro opinions of themselves.

But human cultures are, fortunately, tough and resilient, and though Bunyoro's private history is no doubt unique, the strains to which it has been subjected have been suffered in some degree by many other cultures. It has been part of the aim of this book to show that Nyoro culture is still a vital one, and there are no real grounds for supposing that it will cease to be so. It is, all the time, both changing and adapting itself to change: even during the short span of my fieldwork progressive change was taking place, and no doubt Bunyoro today is not quite the same as it was when I last saw it a few years ago. And this persisting process of adaptation, disruptive and painful though it often is, implies the continuous creation of a new social synthesis whose character is not resoluble to a mere sum of preexisting cultural elements hitherto uncombined. Any culture, any society, is a unique phenomenon at any point in time, and a great part of the fascination of anthropology lies in this fact. And just as it has been one of the themes of this book that Bunyoro's past is contained in its present, so, it may be presumed, its present will be incapsulated in its future. If the researches of social anthropologists today can help future inquirers into social institutions to understand them better, their work will not have been wasted. Social anthropology is no less valuable when it changes into social history.

Recommended Reading

General Reading on Culture Area

FALLERS, L. A., 1956, *Bantu Bureaucracy*. Cambridge, Eng.: Heffer & Sons.

An account of the social and political organization of the Soga, an important Bantu people in Uganda, some of whose territory is said formerly to have been subject to Bunyoro. The book shows the effects of a European administration on a traditional political system, and describes, in particular, the changed role of the chiefs.

FORTES, M., and E. E. EVANS-PRITCHARD (Eds.), 1940, *African Political Systems*. London: Oxford University Press.

Describes the political organization of eight African tribal societies, of which five are Bantu, and two, Ankole and the Bantu of Kavirondo, are members of the Interlacustrine group, to which Bunyoro belongs.

KUPER, H., 1947, *An African Aristocracy*. London: Oxford University Press.

A graphic account of the Bantu kingdom of the Swazi of South Africa. Though a long way from Uganda, the state described shows interesting parallels and contrasts with Bunyoro.

MAIR, L. P., 1934, *An African People in the Twentieth Century*. London: Routledge & Sons.

An account of the social and political organization of the Ganda, Bunyoro's powerful neighbors to the southeast.

ROSCOE, REV. J., 1911, *The Baganda*. London: Macmillan.

The earliest full account of the neighboring kingdom. The author spent many years in Buganda as an Anglican missionary, and his account of its traditional culture contains much of comparative interest for the student of Bunyoro.

RICHARDS, A. I. (Ed.), 1954, *Economic Development and Tribal Change*. Cambridge, Eng.: Heffer & Sons.

An interesting account, by various authors, of the social effects of the development of a cash economy and consequent labor immigration on the traditional way of life of the Ganda and some neighboring peoples.

SELIGMAN, C. G., 1957, *Races of Africa*. London: Oxford University Press.

A useful introductory account of the various peoples of the African continent. There are two chapters about the Bantu-speaking peoples, and some account of the Interlacustrine group, of which the Nyoro are members.

RICHARDS, A. I. (Ed.), 1960, *East African Chiefs*. London: Faber and Faber.

Descriptions by social anthropologists of a number of contemporary East African political systems, including some in Uganda. The chapter on Bunyoro, by the present author, provides a more detailed account of modern Nyoro chiefs than could be given in this book.

MAIR, L., 1962, *Primitive Government*. Penguin Books.

A detailed discussion of the various institutional means through which social and political order were traditionally maintained among various East African peoples, including the Nyoro.

Specific References to Bunyoro

There are references to Bunyoro in a great many books and articles by explorers, missionaries, administrators, and others. Only a few of the more important are listed here.

BAKER, SIR S., 1867, *Albert Nyanza, Great Basin of the Nile*. London: Macmillan.

Describes Baker's first visit to Bunyoro, and his relations with the Nyoro king, Kamurasi.

BEATTIE, J. H. M., 1958, *Nyoro Kinship, Marriage and Affinity*. London: Oxford University Press. (International African Institute Memorandum)

A detailed account of the terminology of Nyoro kinship and affinity, and of the social relationships which these terms imply.

FISHER, (MRS.) A. B., 1911, *Twilight Tales of the Black Baganda*. London: Marshall Brothers.

Contains a very full account in English of Nyoro myth and traditional history.

JOHNSTON, SIR H., 1902, *The Uganda Protectorate* (2 vols.). London: Hutchinson & Company.

> An early description of Uganda and its peoples. Volume II contains a brief account of the Nyoro.

LUGARD, SIR F. D., 1893, *The Rise of Our East African Empire*. London: Blackwood & Sons.

————, 1900, *The Story of the Uganda Protectorate*. London: Marshall.

> Both of these books contain references to Nyoro-European relations during the last years of the nineteenth century.

ROSCOE, REV. J., 1915, *The Northern Bantu*. Cambridge, Eng.: Cambridge University Press.

————, 1922, *The Soul of Central Africa*. London: Cassell & Company.

> These two books contain chapters on the Nyoro.

————, 1923, *The Bakitara or Banyoro*. Cambridge, Eng.: Cambridge University Press.

> The first full-length study of the Nyoro. It contains interesting if not wholly accurate chapters on the kingship, customs connected with cattle, and other matters.

SPEKE, J. H., 1863, *Journal of the Discovery of the Source of the Nile*. London: Blackwood & Sons.

> Describes the first European contact with Bunyoro.